ASTD Competency Study

ASTD Competency Study

The Training & Development Profession Redefined

Justin Arneson
William J. Rothwell
Jennifer Naughton

16 15 14 13 1 2 3 4 5

ASTD Press is an internationally renowned source of insightful and practical information on workplace learning, performance, and professional development.

ASTD Press
1640 King Street Box 1443
Alexandria, VA 22313-1443 USA

Ordering information: Books published by ASTD Press can be purchased by visiting ASTD's website at store.astd.org or by calling 800.628.2783 or 703.683.8100.

Library of Congress Control Number: 2013936148

ISBN-10: 1-56286-866-7
ISNB-13: 978-1-56286-866-6
e-ISBN: 978-1-60728-544-1

ASTD Press Editorial Staff:
Director: Glenn Saltzman
Manager and Editor, ASTD Press: Ashley McDonald
Community of Practice Manager, Career Development: Jennifer Homer
Editorial Assistant: Sarah Cough
Text Design: Abella Publishing Services, Inc.
Cover Design: Lon Levy

Printed by Versa Press, Inc., East Peoria, IL, www.versapress.com

TABLE OF CONTENTS

PREFACE

For more than 30 years, ASTD has created competency models that define standards of excellence and professionalism in the training and development field. From the first study conducted in 1978 to the more recent one in 2004, ASTD's competency studies illuminate the knowledge, skills, abilities, and behaviors that are required for success in the profession.

Your role as a facilitator of learning, business partner, and developer of the world's workforce has never been more critical than it is today. Senior leaders rely on your expertise and entrust you to build the capability of the organization's human capital. They know that having a knowledgeable and skilled workforce will enable the organization to compete and succeed in today's global economy.

To help your organization and those you serve be successful, building your own competencies in the profession should be a critical part of your professional and career development journey. This Study highlights the most critical foundational and business competencies required for professional success, and the Areas of Expertise (AOEs) that are fundamental in this field.

As we unveil the *ASTD Competency Study: The Training & Development Profession Redefined*, we owe deep thanks to our research partners at HumRRO, Mike Hamm for his assistance in the survey research work, Dr. William Rothwell for his continued contributions to the ASTD competency studies, and the team at DDI who set a tremendous foundation in 2004 upon which this new Study was built.

I encourage you to use the results of this Study to identify the major trends in learning. Understand the changes in the foundational competencies and AOEs, determine which ones require more focused attention, and chart your own professional development plan to fill any gaps.

All of us in the profession have an incredible opportunity to help organizations succeed like never before. Very few occupations can say they are poised to have such a dramatic impact on building individual capabilities and contributing to organizational success as the training field can. Please let us know how we can continue to help you thrive and grow in your career.

Thank you for your engagement with ASTD and our global community of training professionals.

Tony Bingham

Tony Bingham
President and CEO
ASTD

ABOUT THE AUTHORS

Justin Arneson

Justin Arneson is currently a research scientist with CPP, Inc. His responsibilities include planning, directing, and implementing the research and development plans for assessment products at CPP, Inc. Prior to that he was a senior scientist with the Human Resources Research Organization. He has 10 years of experience in job analysis, competency modeling, and test development. He holds a PhD from the University of Minnesota in industrial/organizational psychology.

William J. Rothwell

William J. Rothwell, PhD, SPHR, is the president of Rothwell & Associates, Inc. (www.rothwellandassociates.com) and professor in the Workforce Education and Development Program at the University Park campus of Penn State University. As a researcher he has been involved with the last five competency studies conducted by ASTD. In 2012 he won ASTD's prestigious Distinguished Contribution to Workplace Learning and Performance Award. He is author of 81 books and 250 articles in the field and had 20 years of experience in the HRD field in government and in business before becoming a college professor in 1993. He received his PhD from the University of Illinois at Urbana-Champaign in 1985. He bears lifetime certification as an SPHR.

Jennifer A. Naughton

Jennifer Naughton is the senior director of Competencies & Credentialing at ASTD. In this capacity she is responsible for providing the vision and direction for the ASTD Competency Model and credentialing initiatives, including the Certified Professional in Learning and Performance (CPLP) certification program. She is a people systems architect with 20 years of experience in the field whose passion is providing competency modeling, assessment development, and human resource strategy expertise to address organizational challenges. She has authored and co-authored numerous articles on human capital related topics. She holds a master's degree in human resource development from The George Washington University and is a Senior Professional of Human Resources (SPHR), as recognized by the HR Certification Institute.

EXECUTIVE SUMMARY

The 2004 *ASTD Competency Study: Mapping the Future* was built on three decades of ASTD competency research, and the model associated with it defined the profession in context of its strategic contribution to organizational performance. The 2013 *ASTD Competency Study: The Training & Development Profession Redefined* follows the research-based professional competencies path blazed by the 2004 publication. Like its predecessor, the 2013 Study identifies key trends and drivers that are expected to have the greatest effect on current and future practice and includes:

- a broad inventory of topics that training and development professionals need to know to be successful in today's rapidly changing business environment
- specific key actions practitioners must *take* and what they must *do* to succeed.

What is different about the 2013 publication is that its recommendations are directly tied to unprecedented global changes, including these four specific factors:

- a once-in-a-generation global economic collapse followed by four years of a recession
- rapidly advancing technologies that have turned smartphones, tablets, and other mobile devices into preferred substitutes for desktop and laptop computers
- major demographic shifts in the workforce
- unrelenting globalization of the business environment.

Key Trends Shaping the Profession

The principal goal of the 2013 Competency Study was to update the knowledge, skills, abilities, and behaviors first identified in the ASTD 2004 Competency Study. To maintain consistency, researchers mirrored the 2004 research methodology. Researchers also drew conclusions based on feedback from multiple stakeholder groups and diverse sets of data.

This work resulted in the identification of eight key trends currently driving change for training and development professionals. A brief discussion of these trends and drivers follows.

Advances in Technology and Internet Capability

Advances in the speed, storage capacity, functionality, and user interfaces of popular electronic devices such as smartphones, tablets, and other mobile devices have made anywhere, anytime, anyplace learning possible. In fact, these devices have become expected training delivery platforms that serve as options for desktop and laptop computers.

Advances in Software Applications

Rapidly developing software applications are expanding the training and development professional's role to more than a deliverer of training. This much more expansive role requires an ability to identify, select, and apply the appropriate software application for a specific learning opportunity. This skill will become a requirement for both initial employment and career advancement. Another notable trend is the increasing use of social software applications for sharing knowledge and information.

Growing Adoption of Mobile Devices for Learning

Clearly, training and development professionals are increasingly designing and delivering training to suit an ever-expanding list of mobile devices, including smartphones, tablets, and e-readers. The 2012 *State of the Industry Report (SOIR)* reported that 28 percent of the respondents noted that their organizations make internal learning content available via mobile devices (ASTD, 48). The *SOIR* further characterized the "ubiquity of mobile devices" and their increasing appropriateness for delivering learning solutions as a key factor in "changing the world and our experience of it."

A Culture of Connectivity and Information Sharing

Constant 24/7 connection, and instant communication and interaction with co-workers, colleagues, friends, and family around the world is now the cultural norm; a reality that the learning functions of organizations cannot ignore. Those charged with training this new generation of connected learners will need updated knowledge, skills, abilities, and behaviors.

Increased Ability to Use and Collect "Big Data"

Advances in technology also underpin a move by most companies to make decisions based heavily on business intelligence and data analytics, or "big data." Clearly, training and development professionals need to understand what's behind these business metrics and how organizational leaders use them to allocate resources. Moreover, these professionals must be able to select the metrics that have meaning and value to their organization and its leaders.

Shifting Demographics in the Workforce

Training and development professionals face a challenging array of employee demographics. There is the generation of workers who have grown up in a culture of connectivity and social networking who fully *expect* to change jobs many times during their careers. These same workers also insist on being offered appropriate tools and opportunities that facilitate self-improvement and career advancement. In contrast, there are older workers with a different set of priorities and career expectations, many of whom are staying in the workforce due to the lingering effect of the 2008 economic collapse.

Increasing Globalization

A growing interconnected global workforce of more than 3 billion workers represents an opportunity for training and development professionals to demonstrate their value and relevance as a new generation takes the reins of leadership. As noted by ASTD CEO Tony Bingham and co-author Marcia Connor in their book *The New Social Learning*, "the next generation of workers is coming into the workforce with . . . a global-mindedness their elders never would have imagined" (150-151).

Economic Volatility and Uncertainty

Training and development professionals also face added pressure to demonstrate value, relevance, and bottom-line impact even as organizations recover from the 2008 economic meltdown. Most organizations will continue to take a "do more with less" approach and choose not to replace lost workers despite prospects for a brighter economic future.

Implications for Training and Development Professionals

Depending on their roles, work assignments, and the cultures of the companies that employ them, individual training and development professionals must be prepared to address these drivers and trends head-on in order to be successful. These needed actions include taking steps to:

- connect the strategic needs and priorities of the training function to those of the organization
- find innovative and creative ways to deliver training programs that take advantage of the best and most appropriate technologies
- adapt to changing demographics that include multiple generations in the workforce who have new expectations about learning and work
- design and deliver training programs that are accessible anywhere, anytime
- be adept at analyzing and converting business data into insights and actions for improving training
- scan for existing and emerging technologies and understand if and how they address training and development challenges and opportunities.

The ultimate effect of the specific trends and drivers previously noted will shape the profession for years to come. But perhaps the most important factor to note is that the prevalent use of knowledge-sharing and collaborative technologies—including those geared toward social and informal learning—means a fundamental change in the training and development professional's role. The ability to identify, select, and apply the appropriate learning technology for a specific learning opportunity or challenge will be an expected skill.

Other Critical Implications

Learning management system (LMS) software applications for the administration, documentation, tracking, reporting, and delivery of training are increasingly important tools for training and development professionals. The key capabilities of LMSs—including support for blended learning approaches that enable self-guided and collaborative learning communities—require that training professionals work with technical experts to implement and administer these systems and keep up with the constant changes in LMS capabilities.

Many organizations now weave employee engagement and learning throughout their talent management process. The practice helps maintain a robust pipeline of coached candidates for key roles, helps develop workforce capability in anticipation of need, and makes knowledge sharing part of succession planning.

Training and development professionals must learn to convert consolidated talent management data that includes all aspects of the performance management cycle into insights and actions for designing and delivering instructional programs.

Finally, training professionals should take the following actions to create a culture of strong learning and business alignment:

- Develop a business case for learning that focuses on the training function's benefits.
- Include business leaders in the strategic planning process to identify their specific needs.
- Develop benchmarks and scorecards to measure goals developed in the strategy-planning phase.
- Continue to evaluate learning events and their return on mission.
- Make alignment a priority and hold those responsible for implementation accountable.

A New Model Suited for Today and the Future

The principal goal of the 2013 ASTD Competency Study was to update the knowledge, skills, abilities, and behaviors first identified in the 2004 study. The areas of technology, measuring and evaluating, and talent management were found to be outdated (some substantially) and required updating. In addition, the structure of the 2013 Model was changed to reflect a move away from roles and a hierarchal structure in the AOEs. The specifics of these changes are outlined on the following page.

The 2013 ASTD Competency Model

A competency model is a high-level graphic depiction of the knowledge, skills, abilities, and behaviors (or competencies) required for success in a particular profession or job—in this case the training and development profession.

The iconic ASTD Competency Model graphic (a pyramid) used in 2004 (see Figure 1) is different from the two-structure graphic model used for the 2013 Competency Model (see Figure 2). The base structure of the 2013 Model contains the Foundational Competencies. The second structure—the pentagon that sits on the base—contains the specific Areas of Expertise (AOEs). The new 2013 graphic eliminates the four roles—learning strategist, business partner, project manager, and professional specialist—depicted in the 2004 Model.

Figure 1: 2004 Model

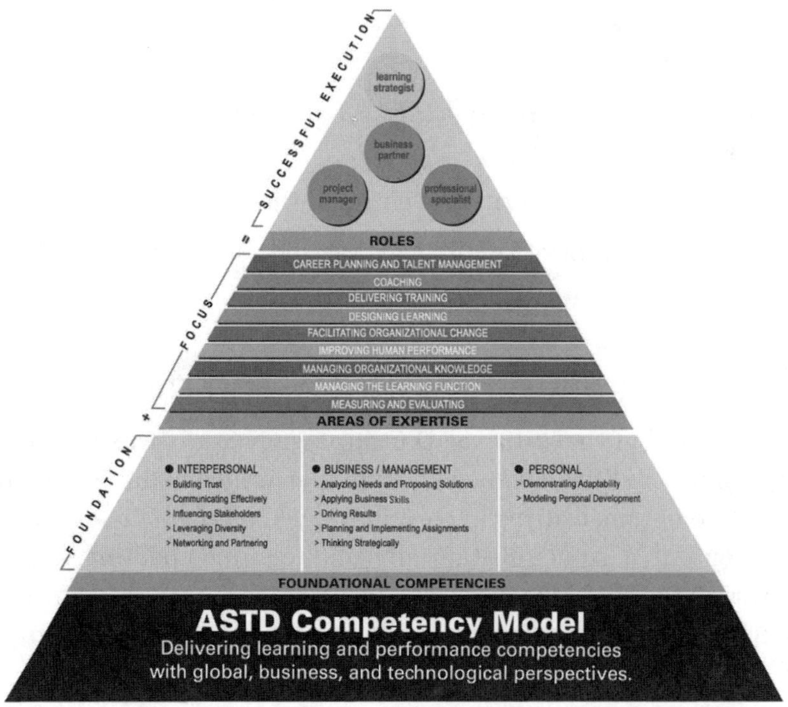

Foundational Competencies are the bedrock competencies used as the foundation to build more specific competencies. These competencies are important regardless of the specific organization, industry, or AOE in which a practitioner practices. The 10 *Areas of Expertise* (or AOEs) in the 2013 Competency Model contain the specialized, functional knowledge and skill sets needed by training and development professionals for success. Detailed definitions and key knowledge and action statements for both the Foundational Competencies and the AOEs accompany the high-level graphic model.

2013 Foundational Competencies

The Foundational Competencies in the 2013 Model now reflect an additional emphasis on the areas of technology literacy, adopting a global mindset, demonstrating emotional intelligence, developing dual industry knowledge, and being innovative. These are characteristics and proficiencies that training and development professionals must demonstrate to be successful in the current business environment.

The six Foundational Competencies in the 2013 Model include: Business Skills, Global Mindset, Industry Knowledge, Interpersonal Skills, Personal Skills, and Technology Literacy. Each of these Foundational Competencies is discussed in the sections that follow.

Figure 2: New Competency Model

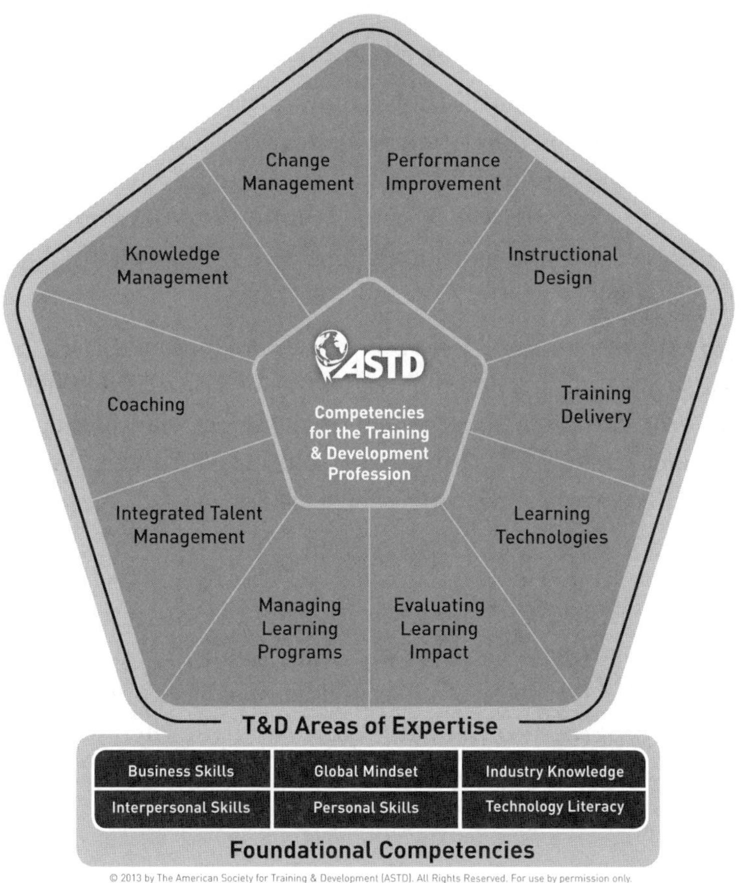

Business Skills

- ***Analyzing Needs and Proposing Solutions***—Identifies and understands business issues and client needs, problems, and opportunities; compares data from different sources to draw conclusions; uses effective approaches for choosing a course of action or developing appropriate solutions; takes action that is consistent with available facts, constraints, and probable consequences.
- ***Applying Business Skills***—Understands the organization's business strategies, key metrics, and financial goals; uses economic, financial, and organizational data to build and document the business case for investing in learning solutions; uses business terminology when communicating with others.
- ***Driving Results***—Identifies opportunities for improvement and sets well-defined goals related to training and development solutions; orchestrates efforts and measures progress; strives to achieve/exceed goals and produces exceptional results.
- ***Planning and Implementing Assignments***—Develops action plans, obtains resources, and completes assignments in a timely manner to ensure that training and development goals are achieved.
- ***Thinking Strategically***—Understands internal and external factors that affect training and development in organizations; keeps abreast of trends and anticipates opportunities to add value to the business; operates from a systems perspective in creating training and development strategies; creates training and development strategies that are in alignment with business goals.
- ***Applying Innovation***—Uses new resources, methods, tools, or content to advance training and development; incorporates or applies new thinking or new techniques into training and development solutions; applies existing techniques in new ways to enhance solutions, including those designed to more fully engage and support the learner.

Global Mindset

- Appreciates and leverages the capabilities, insights, and ideas of all individuals; works effectively with individuals from different generations who have diverse styles, abilities, motivations, and/or backgrounds; works effectively across borders and cultures given the increasingly global workforce.

Industry Knowledge

- Actively scans and assesses information on current and emerging trends in the training and development industry; develops and maintains knowledge of other industries, as appropriate.

Interpersonal Skills

- ***Building Trust***—Interacts with others in a way that gives them confidence in one's intentions and those of the organization.
- ***Communicating Effectively***—Expresses thoughts, feelings, and ideas in a clear, concise, and compelling manner in both individual and group situations; actively listens to others; adjusts style to capture the attention of the audience; develops and deploys targeted communication strategies that inform and build support.
- ***Influencing Stakeholders***—Sells the value of learning or the recommended solution as a way of improving organizational performance; gains commitment to solutions that will improve individual, team, and organizational performance.
- ***Networking and Partnering***—Develops and uses a network of collaborative relationships with internal and external contacts to leverage the training and development strategy in a way that facilitates the accomplishment of business results.
- ***Emotional Intelligence***—Perceives the emotional state of one's own self and others accurately and uses that information to help guide effective decision making and build positive working relationships.

Personal Skills

- ***Demonstrating Adaptability***—Maintains effectiveness when experiencing major changes in work tasks, the work environment, or conditions affecting the organization (for example, economic, political, cultural, or technological); remains open to new people, thoughts, and approaches; adjusts effectively to work within new work structures, processes, requirements, or cultures.
- ***Modeling Personal Development***—Actively identifies new areas for one's own personal learning; regularly creates and takes advantage of learning opportunities; applies newly gained knowledge and skill on the job.

Technology Literacy

- Demonstrates an awareness of or comfort with existing, new, and emerging technologies; demonstrates a practical understanding of technology trends; identifies opportunities to leverage technology in order to accomplish learning tasks and achieve business goals.

Areas of Expertise

The 2013 ASTD Competency Model includes important changes to the AOEs. Specifically, the 2013 Competency Model provides updates to Designing Learning (now Instructional Design) and Delivering Training (now Training Delivery), as well as new content on informal learning methods, social media, and leveraging technology. Measurement and Evaluation (now Evaluating Learning Impact) incorporates learning analytics. Managing Organizational Knowledge (Knowledge Management) no longer includes activities typically carried out by information technology. Career Planning and Talent Management (now Integrated Talent Management) better reflects integrated talent management activities. Finally, Learning Technologies was added as an AOE. The following are the definitions of the 10 AOEs in the 2013 ASTD Competency Model:

- ***Performance Improvement***—Applies a systematic process of discovering and analyzing human performance gaps; plans for future improvements in human performance; designs and develops solutions to close performance gaps; partners with the customer when identifying the opportunity and the solution; implements the solution; monitors the change; evaluates the results.
- ***Instructional Design***—Designs, creates, and develops informal and formal learning solutions to meet organizational needs; analyzes and selects the most appropriate strategy, methodologies, and technologies to maximize the learning experience and impact.
- ***Training Delivery***—Delivers informal and formal learning solutions in a manner that engages the learner and produces desired outcomes; manages and responds to learner needs; ensures that the learning is made available in effective platforms and delivered in a timely and effective manner.
- ***Learning Technologies***—Identifies, selects, and applies a variety of learning technologies; adapts learning technologies; matches the appropriate technology to the specific learning opportunity or challenge at hand.
- ***Evaluating Learning Impact***—Gathers, organizes, and analyzes information regarding the impact of learning solutions against key business drivers; presents the information in a way that is meaningful to the organization; uses learning metrics and analytics to inform organizational decision making.
- ***Managing Learning Programs***—Provides leadership to execute the organization's strategy; plans, monitors, and adjusts training and development projects or activities.

- ***Integrated Talent Management***—Builds an organization's culture, engagement, capability, and capacity through the implementation and integration of talent acquisition, employee development, retention, and deployment processes; ensures that these processes are aligned to organizational goals.
- ***Coaching***—Uses an interactive process to help individuals develop rapidly and produce results; improves others' ability to set goals, take action, make better decisions, and make full use of their natural strengths.
- ***Knowledge Management***—Captures, distributes, and archives intellectual capital in a way that encourages knowledge-sharing and collaboration in the organization.
- ***Change Management***—Applies structured approaches to shift individuals, teams, and organizations from a current state to a desired state.

Applying the ASTD Competency Model

While the 2013 Competency Model pinpoints critical knowledge, skills, abilities, and behaviors for training and development professionals, the real value is in its application.

The various human resources (HR) systems that can be built around the competencies outlined in the report are highlighted in Figure 3. Training and development professionals need to work within their organizations to incorporate both the Foundational Competencies and AOEs into their own HR systems to create one integrated system with a common set of competencies. Because the same competencies and AOEs underpin all of the systems, each part operates more efficiently and ultimately saves training costs.

Other Stakeholder Uses and Benefits

For chief learning officers (CLOs) and other training and development managers, the 2013 ASTD Competency Model can serve as a template for success today and in the future. The Model may be used to determine which competencies and AOEs are appropriate for a unit's training and development professionals and as a way to encourage these professionals to expand and enhance their skills.

Figure 3: Integrated HR Systems

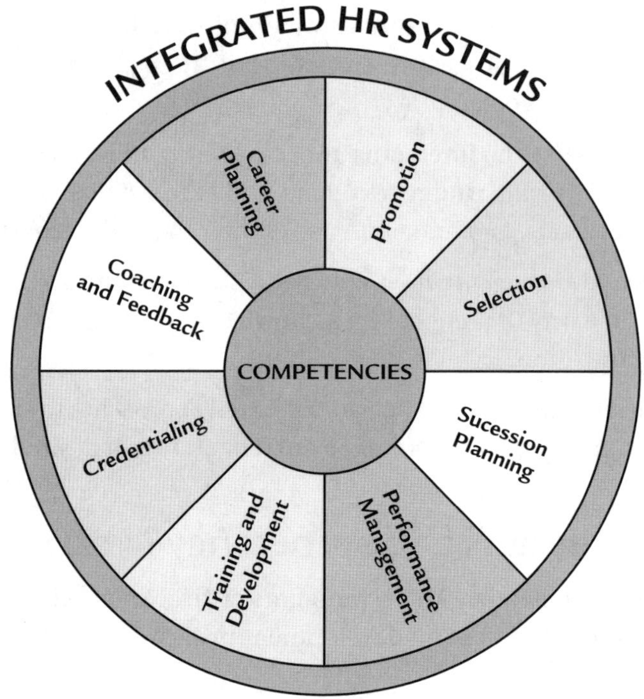

How Organizations Can Use the Model

Organizations can use the ASTD Competency Model to improve performance in a number of ways including:

- Performance management: The ASTD Competency Model provides the foundation and specific language for a comprehensive or upgraded performance management program regardless of the type of assessment being developed.
- Strategy alignment: The Model is an excellent resource to help build a scorecard to ensure that the training and development function meets the strategic and operational needs of the business and that the right skills to accomplish the mission both now and in the future are in place.
- Benchmarking: Learning leaders and managers can use the Model to build a comprehensive benchmarking assessment tool to ensure that resources are used and managed effectively.
- Managing talent: Organizations can use the Model as a road map to develop comprehensive assessment tools for both selection and development purposes. It is also an appropriate tool to help leaders manage the talent in their training function.

Uses for Individual Contributors

The ASTD Competency Model clearly describes what competencies professionals should have today and in the future. As such, it provides training and development professionals a broad overview of the profession and how their job fits into the full range of professional competencies. In addition, the Model can be used to target individual skill development needs or as a basis for career exploration for learning executives, external consultants, and subject matter experts.

Educational Uses

The competency and AOE definitions provided by the ASTD Competency Model are also excellent tools for educators to evaluate current curricula and to take stock of their learners' interests, planning and evaluating new or existing course offerings, guiding student development paths, or as the focal point for prioritizing lifelong learning.

Serving the ASTD Mission

The 2013 ASTD Competency Model redefines training and development competencies in light of profound changes in technology, the economy, and new expectations that organizations have about the contribution of employee training.

ASTD's mission—to empower professionals to develop knowledge and skills successfully—drives our commitment to identifying competencies in the training and development profession. Practitioners and organizations must take advantage of the opportunity before them and invest in development and growth. The benefits of this commitment will result in higher levels of expertise and will drive renewed respect for the training and development profession.

CHAPTER 1

The Value of the ASTD Competency Model

Since the 2004 publication of ASTD's Competency Study, training and development practitioners have weathered a tsunami of change that has forever altered the context and nature of their role and challenged fundamental assumptions about professional practice.

As a result, these practitioners must now demonstrate their organizational value and relevancy more than ever by engaging with a host of rapidly advancing technological capabilities (particularly digital, mobile, and social technology). At the same time, these professionals must adapt to once-in-a-generation economic conditions while coping with shifting cultural and social expectations on an unprecedented global scale.

As an organization focused on empowering professionals to develop knowledge and skills successfully, ASTD is committed to presenting a clear picture of the current and future state of the profession. The 2004 *ASTD Competency Study: Mapping the Future*—a report built on three decades of ASTD competency research—contained a new model that defined the profession in the context of its strategic contribution to organizational performance. For a summary of prior ASTD competency studies and related key findings, see appendix A.

This updated 2013 Competency Stu[illegible]*etency Study: The Training & Development Profession Redefined*) f[illegible] blazed by the 2004 publication and other previous studies. In [illegible]g built on a solid research foundation (see sidebar on page 3 an[illegible] and C), it identifies trends and drivers expected to have the greatest impact on current and future practice. Furthermore, the updated study provides practitioners with:

- a broad inventory of topics that training and development professionals need to know to be successful in today's rapidly changing business environment
- specific key actions practitioners must *take* and what they must *do* to succeed.

What is different about the 2013 publication is that its recommendations are directly tied to unprecedented global change including these four specific factors:

- a once-in-a-generation global economic collapse and four years of a recession
- rapidly advancing technologies, including digital, mobile, and social
- major demographic shifts in the workforce
- unrelenting globalization of the business environment.

These factors have had a seismic impact on long-held assumptions about talent management, evaluating and measuring learning impact, employee engagement, and workplace expectations. Practitioners cannot afford to ignore such a clarion call to take action now to maintain competitive advantage. That's why the competencies outlined in this publication are so critical for today's training and development practitioner. These updated competencies include:

- staying current with new and emerging technologies and the ability to match the right technology to a specific learning opportunity or challenge
- becoming more a facilitator of learning, content curator, information manager, and builder of learning communities and less a deliverer of training
- developing an understanding that learning is a process—not a discrete event—that engages learners in a variety of ways over time using formal and informal approaches
- developing an ability to leverage the learning styles and preferences of new generations entering the workforce and capturing the knowledge of those leaving it
- understanding the role and contribution of the learning function in integrated talent management to help build organizational capability

- contributing to performance management to proactively meet the development needs of an increasingly global workforce
- using metrics and data analysis that are meaningful to business and that accurately measure the effectiveness and efficiency of training and development
- aligning training and development activities to organizational business strategies to demonstrate return on mission, especially during challenging times.

Methodology Overview

The principal goal of the 2013 Competency Study was to identify any needed changes or updates to essential practitioner knowledge, skills, abilities, and behaviors that were first identified in the 2004 Competency Study.

To maintain consistency between the 2004 and 2013 studies researchers mirrored the 2004 research methodology. As in 2004, data-gathering approaches were varied, and conclusions were drawn based on feedback from multiple stakeholder groups and from the use of diverse sets of data.

Essentially, researchers found that gaps had developed in the years separating the two competency studies. For data collection details for the 2013 study, see appendix B.

Review of Research Approach

Phase 1: Review of the literature. Recent publications in the training and development field were reviewed as well as products and materials from ASTD's archives. The review process also extended to the feedback and reports from the ASTD Certification Institute's Certified Professional in Learning and Performance (CPLP®) testing program. This activity produced big-picture conclusions about the direction of the training and development profession and identified what knowledge, skills, abilities, and behaviors will be needed to meet future challenges.

Phase 2: Data collection. This phase involved collecting detailed day-to-day job data from training and development professionals. Leaders in the field were interviewed and questioned about both global trends and current and future needs of the profession. In addition, "in-the-trench" practitioners were interviewed to develop a more accurate picture of the specific behaviors that contribute to successful job performance. Furthermore, social media and discussion boards were also used to solicit targeted feedback. This enabled more robust discussion from a wider cross section of senior practitioners.

Phase 3: Validation. A survey was developed using all the information learned in phases 1 and 2. This comprehensive survey was then administered to the entire ASTD membership base. Participants were asked to rate the importance of each of the identified Areas of Expertise along with their component behaviors. This methodology ensured that the content had broad applicability.

Other Validation Methodology

A core component of the research for the 2013 Competency Study was strong reliance on subject matter experts to provide feedback on any perceived limitations or deficiencies in the 2004 Competency Study. In-depth interviews were conducted with nearly two dozen strategically oriented thought leaders who provided a broad landscape view of the profession concerning its current and future directions. More detailed content was obtained through one-on-one interviews and focus groups conducted with nearly 50 frontline CPLP practitioners with expertise in one or more Areas of Expertise.

Why Use Competency Models?

Competency models are powerful organizational tools because these models go beyond the more superficial *what people do* information provided by traditional job descriptions and job analysis approaches, especially in terms of how they are able to link individual performance goals to organizational goals and strategies. (See Campion, Fink, Ruggeberg, Carr, Phillips, & Odman, 2011.)

Ultimately, competency models enable organizations to identify and develop promising performers by providing a target set of defined knowledge, skills, abilities, and behaviors needed for success. Without these identified targets, it's hard to know for sure what workforce characteristics are most effective. As the old saying goes, "If you don't know what you want, you don't know what you'll get."

The major benefit of the 2013 ASTD Competency Model is that it provides a clearly defined set of knowledge areas, skills, abilities, and behaviors for the entire training and development profession.

ASTD Model Advantages

The ASTD Competency Model is an occupational model. In other words, it defines the competencies needed across the entire scope of the profession versus those needed for a subset of jobs in a single organization.

The ASTD Competency Model has both strategic and practical benefits. From a strategic perspective, it helps to advance the training and development field by:

- defining the profession and codifying it
- structuring consistent ways to communicate about the profession
- informing quality standards for professional practice
- providing a foundation for professional certification.

From a practical perspective, current and future training professionals and their managers and leaders will be able to use the Competency Model to:

- better understand the field
- identify the types of jobs in the profession that best match their skills and interests
- become certified in the profession
- select, appraise, reward, develop, coach, or improve the performance of career training and development staff
- find insight into what training and development competencies are needed by line operating managers and subject matter experts who conduct ad hoc or informal training
- link individual performance goals to organizational goals and strategies for individuals in the learning function
- focus and unify ways that organizations build their training and development staff.

ASTD Model Limitations

The ASTD Competency Model is not designed to be an out-of-the-box solution or one-size fits-all Model. It may require customization to be useful in specific corporate or organizational cultures and certain industries or industry segments. In these situations, assistance from an expert who is familiar with how to customize competency models is recommended.

Furthermore, the ASTD Competency Model does not describe the competencies required of learners. In addition, its use may be more appropriate for certain national cultures or geographic locations than others.

Ultimate Value of ASTD Competency Models

ASTD has produced eight studies of practitioner roles and competencies (including this one) over the past 30 years. These studies have been used by ASTD to support professional development curricula. Furthermore, they have helped ASTD lead the profession by providing findings about the essential competencies needed for success.*

However, the ultimate benefit of the Model may be its value as a quantifiable tool to help training and development practitioners showcase their business relevance and to demonstrate the real contributions they make to organizational performance. Still, the Model is only a tool waiting to be used. To make the best use of its benefits, individual practitioners must take responsibility for their own professional and career development using a tool like this Model; otherwise, the publication of the updated ASTD Competency Model will have little impact.

So the challenge is clearly framed: Practitioners and organizations must take advantage of the opportunity before them and invest in development and growth. The benefits of this commitment will result in higher levels of training and development expertise and, at the same time, drive renewed respect from internal and external customers, clients, and colleagues.

* A complete accounting of these previous competency studies is provided in appendix A. To order publications mentioned in appendix A, go to www.astd.org/store.

CHAPTER 2

What Key Trends Drive the Field?

Training and development professionals face a work environment that is radically different from the one they faced when the 2004 Competency Study was published.

Proof of the dizzying pace of technological advancements in that short span of years is no further away than the mobile devices we use every day. It is no wonder that these versatile devices and the powerful technology enabling their use are all closely aligned to the major industry drivers and trends identified by the 2013 ASTD Competency Study research.

Specifically, this research resulted in the identification of eight key trends currently driving change for training and development professionals. A brief discussion of these trends and drivers follows.

Advances in Technology and Internet Capability

Advances in the speed, storage capacity, functionality, and user interfaces of popular electronic devices have created expectations of similar performance in technology used for training. These advances have turned smartphones, tablets, and other mobile devices into preferred substitutes for desktop and laptop computers. They have made anywhere, anytime learning not only possible but expected.

Advances in Software Applications

Rapidly developing software applications are expanding the training and development professional's role from a deliverer of training to a much more expansive role that includes an ability to identify, select, and apply the appropriate software application for a specific learning opportunity. This skill will become an expected, even required ability for both initial employment and for career advancement. Another notable trend is the use of social software applications and their increasing use for sharing knowledge and information.

Growing Adoption of Mobile Devices for Learning

Training and development professionals are taking up the challenge of designing and delivering training to suit an ever-expanding list of mobile devices, including smartphones, tablets, and e-readers.

According to the 2012 *State of the Industry Report*, the "ubiquity of mobile devices seems to have created a perfect environment for delivering learning solutions to our workforce where or when they need it. Mobile technology is changing the world and our experience of it." The report indicates that many companies are at least experimenting with delivering mobile content as 28 percent of the study respondents reported that their organization makes internal learning content available via mobile devices (ASTD, 48).

A Culture of Connectivity and Information Sharing

The culture of connectivity is the practice of instant connection, communication, and interaction with others—including co-workers—via social technology. Social technology now provides hundreds of ways to connect, share, and collaborate 24/7 with co-workers, colleagues, friends, and family around the world. This technological reality has created a norm that the learning functions of organizations cannot afford to ignore or easily suppress.

Increased Ability to Use and Collect "Big Data"

Advances in technology also underpin a move by most companies to make decisions based heavily on business intelligence and data analytics or "big data." Clearly, training and development professionals need to understand what's behind these business metrics and how organizational leaders use them to allocate resources. Moreover, these professionals must be able to select the metrics that have meaning and value to their organization and its leaders.

Shifting Demographics

Designing and delivering learning to new generations who have grown up in a culture of connectivity requires new and upgraded skills for the training and development professional. Today's young workers *expect* to change jobs many times during their careers and to be offered the tools and appropriate opportunities that facilitate their self-improvement and career enhancement efforts.

At the other end of the demographic spectrum, the oldest workers are staying longer than expected in the workforce for economic and other reasons. This new workplace reality of multiple generations in the workplace (as many as four) is creating an additional set of challenges for training and development professionals.

Globalization

As of 2005, 3 billion workers were part of a burgeoning global labor pool employed by multinational companies. This interconnected global workforce represents an opportunity for training and development professionals to demonstrate their value and relevance.

As noted in ASTD's 2012 *State of the Industry Report*, "half of the organizations surveyed in 2012 reported being involved in a global learning function or actively planning to do so within three years" (47). These initiatives continue to be strong despite the inherent language and cultural challenges of these efforts and their budgetary impact to organizations.

A global mindset is likely to prevail as a new generation takes the reins of leadership. "The next generation of workers is coming into the workforce with... a global-mindedness their elders never would have imagined," noted Tony Bingham and Marcia Conner in their book, *The New Social Learning* (150-151).

Economic Volatility and Uncertainty

The U.S. economic meltdown that began in 2008 and its lingering effect on economies around the world will continue to limit recovery and growth for most organizations. Even economic powerhouses such as China and India have been negatively affected by the recession in the West.

Organizations in the West responded to the economic setbacks by cutting workers and expenses. Even as the recovery process began, these organizations did not replace workers. Instead, they chose a "do more with less" approach. This added to the pressure to demonstrate value, relevance, and bottom-line impact for all lines of business, especially training.

How These Trends Affect Training Professionals

How the drivers and trends listed above affect individual training and development professionals depends on their roles, work assignments, and the cultures of the companies that employ them. To be successful, they will need to:

- connect the strategic needs and priorities of the training function to those of the organization
- find innovative and creative ways to deliver training programs that take advantage of best and most appropriate technologies
- adapt to changing demographics that include multiple generations in the workforce who have new expectations about learning and work
- design and deliver learning programs that are accessible anywhere, anytime
- be adept at analyzing and converting business data into insights and actions for improving training
- scan for existing and emerging technologies and understand if and how they address training and development challenges and opportunities.

The training and development profession has already been affected by the trends noted previously, and it will continue to be shaped by them for years to come. But one clearly important factor is how knowledge is gained and shared through social media. Customers, employees, and workers of every business and most government agencies will demand targeted interactions and learning choices suited to their individual needs.

Here are some other specific ways that the emergence of these technologies will affect some key competencies of training and development professionals.

Changing Roles

Rapidly developing technologies for creating and sharing learning continue to expand the training and development professional's role from designing and delivering training to include these and other roles:

- facilitator of learning
- content curator
- information manager
- builder of learning communities.

These expanded roles—driven largely by knowledge-sharing and collaborative technologies, including those geared toward social and informal learning—have changed the game for training and development professionals. Being able to identify, select, and apply the appropriate learning technology for a specific learning opportunity or challenge will be expected for both initial employment and career advancement. Furthermore, being able to develop and deliver instruction rapidly and appropriately in technology-based learning environments is a key skill.

Instructional Design and Training Delivery

A 2012 IBM CEO Study of more than 1,700 CEOs and public leaders titled *Leading Through Connections* found that CEOs are increasingly creating more open and collaborative cultures that encourage employees to connect and learn from each other. Collaboration is the number one trait CEOs are seeking in their employees, with 75 percent of the CEOs calling it "critical." Training and development professionals also must learn new ways to design and deliver training that fully leverages these new technologies that permit ubiquitous, collaborative connectivity via a host of devices. It's no longer sufficient to solely rely on classroom-based approaches as a primary way to instruct.

For example, a popular way to engage learners is through gamification, or the use of game design techniques, to draw people into content and to participate in learning. Game techniques can also provide incentives to learn through the use of leader boards and badges that recognize achievement.

A 2011 Gartner Research report notes that by 2015 more than 50 percent of organizations that manage innovation processes will gamify them. Another example is for training professionals to use information assets they have gathered on blogs and other communities and leverage these to form an informational knowledge base for workers. This enables learners to find—in real-time—useful information through informal means without having to rely on more formal instructional events.

Furthermore, given that the "shelf life" of learning materials is now shorter than ever before, instructional designers must adopt new approaches for designing and developing learning content. They are rethinking and re-examining methodologies such as ADDIE and others. They are exploring agile and rapid design, development, and testing approaches, which were once embraced almost exclusively by software developers. Expect these types of approaches to become more common and pervasive in a relatively short span of time.

Managing Learning Systems

Learning management system (LMS) software applications for the administration, documentation, tracking, reporting, and delivery of training are increasingly important tools for learning professionals. Most LMSs are web-based and are used to manage, distribute, and measure the use of learning modules across organizations. LMSs also support blended learning approaches that enable self-guided and collaborative learning communities and can play a role in moving learning from the classroom to the point of need. Using an LMS effectively requires keeping up with constant changes in their capabilities and working with technical experts to implement and administer them.

Integrated Talent Management

Many organizations now weave employee engagement and learning throughout their talent management processes. They create an employee brand to engage people even before they are hired. These organizations maintain a robust pipeline of coached candidates for key roles, develop workforce capability in anticipation of need, and make knowledge sharing part of succession plans. All of these efforts are typically linked by constant communication with employees and frequent opportunities to learn.

Talent management systems are nothing new. What's new and different about them in this new business environment is that independent software and applications are used to silo information into separate functional areas. With the consolidation and forthcoming integration of separate talent management systems, data from all aspects of the performance management cycle will be centralized and available for use. Training and development professionals must learn to be adept at converting user and performance data in these systems into insights and actions for designing and delivering instructional programs and for executive decision-making purposes.

Evaluating Learning Impact

The challenge of showing a direct link between learning programs and business results is always an elusive task for learning professionals. Still, it is a connection that must be made to maintain organizational relevancy and value.

A 2012 ASTD study, *Developing Results: Aligning Learning Goals and Outcomes With Business Performance Measures*, concluded that few organizations successfully link their learning strategy to business results. While noting that the "idea of isolating learning's impact on business versus the influence of other factors may seem like an overwhelmingly arduous task," the study authors emphasized that learning professionals must meet the challenge and become "as astute about business as they are about learning." Organizations meeting this challenge, the study found, had a "strong correlation between goal alignment and market performance" and learning functions that met their own and their organization's goals.

Training professionals striving to create a culture of strong learning and business alignment should take the following actions, according to the study:

- Develop a business case for learning that focuses on the training function's benefits.
- Include business leaders in the strategic planning process to identify their specific needs.
- Develop benchmarks and scorecards to measure goals developed in the strategy-planning phase.
- Continue to evaluate learning events and their return on mission.
- Make alignment a priority and hold those responsible for implementation accountable.

These and other trends that shape business, the economy, and the workforce will continue to influence the practice of training and development in the coming years.

CHAPTER 3

What Were the Results of the Research?

Introduction

The principal goal of the 2013 ASTD Competency Study was to update the knowledge, skills, abilities, and behaviors first identified in the 2004 Competency Study.

Literature reviews, interviews, and surveys found that a number of competencies were outdated (for example, in the areas of technology, measuring and evaluating, and talent management). For these particular areas, some substantial updating was required. Furthermore, the iconic competency model graphic (the pyramid) needed to be simplified.

The surveys conducted for the 2013 Competency Study showed that a majority of respondents (59 percent) reported that Designing Learning (now Instructional Design) or Delivering Training (now Training Delivery) was their primary Area of Expertise (AOE). However, interviews and focus groups with subject matter experts confirmed that very few practitioners spend their entire professional careers devoted solely to design or delivery to the exclusion of other AOEs. (See Table 3.1.) Therefore, a broad model applicable across a number of AOEs was most appropriate.

Table 3.1: Primary Area of Expertise

AOE	Percent
Training Delivery	33.1
Instructional Design	25.7
Managing Learning Programs	15.9
Performance Improvement	7.1
Change Management	5.5
Coaching	4.6
Integrated Talent Management	2.6
Evaluating Learning Impact	2.1
Other	2.1
Knowledge Management	1.4
Total	100

The 2013 ASTD Competency Model

First, here is a refresher. *Competencies* are the knowledge, skills, abilities, and behaviors required for success (in this case, for the training and development profession). They answer the question: What does someone in the training and development profession need to know and do to be successful? By contrast, a *competency model* is a graphic depiction of these competencies.

The ASTD 2013 competency research resulted in a Model with two structures (See Figure 3.1.) The first structure—the base of the Model—contains the Foundational Competencies. The second structure—the pentagon that sits on the base—contains the Areas of Expertise (AOEs).

Foundational Competencies are important to everyone in the field. The Foundational Competencies are the bedrock upon which to build more specific competencies. They are crucial regardless of the specific organization, industry, or AOE in which a practitioner practices.

Areas of Expertise (or *AOEs*) contain the specialized, functional knowledge and skill sets needed for a particular job or industry. In this case, the AOEs are the 10 specialized areas that are required by training and development professionals.

Accompanying the high-level graphic model are the competency dictionaries. These dictionaries contain detailed definitions and key knowledge and action statements for both the Foundational Competencies and the AOEs. To review the dictionaries for the Foundational Competencies and the AOEs, see appendixes D and E, respectively.

New Competency Model

D COMPETENCY MODEL
ng & Development Redefined™

Model Changes Since 2004

Compared to the 2004 Model, in terms of structural changes, there were two. First, the new competency model graphic is no longer in a pyramid shape (see Figure 3.2 for the 2004 version of the Model). The AOEs are now organized into a pentagonal shape so as not to imply a hierarchy. Second, the new graphic

Figure 3.2: 2004 Model

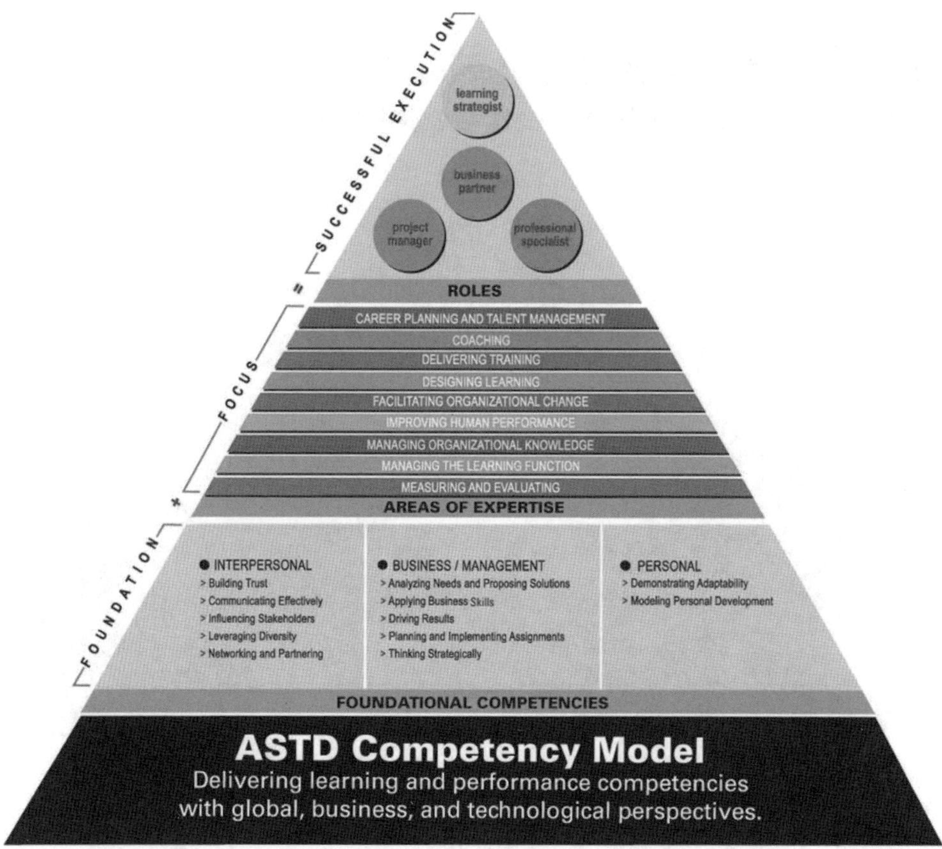

eliminates the four roles—learning strategist, business partner, project manager, and professional specialist—depicted in the 2004 Model (at the top). Research indicated that the roles were non-actionable for most users.

In terms of content, understanding what has changed since 2004 provides important insights and clues into which competencies are emerging, transforming, and increasing in terms of their importance.

This includes the important changes to the Foundational Competencies. Table 3.2 shows the comparison. The Foundational Competencies now reflect an additional emphasis on technology literacy, adopting a global mindset, demonstrating emotional intelligence, developing dual industry knowledge, and being innovative. These are competencies that training and development professionals must demonstrate in the current business environment.

Furthermore, the 2013 ASTD Competency Model includes important changes to the AOEs. Table 3.3 shows the comparison. Specifically, the new Competency Model provides updates to Designing Learning (now Instructional Design) and

Table 3.2: Changes to the Foundational Competencies

Original Name (2004)	New Name (2013)	Description of Content Changes
Business/Management Competencies	Business Skills	Name change
• Analyzing needs and proposing solutions	• Analyzing needs and proposing solutions	No change
• Applying business skills	• Applying business skills	Name change; minor edits
• Driving results	• Driving results	Minor content changes
• Planning and implementing assignments	• Planning and implementing assignments	No change
• Thinking strategically	• Thinking strategically	Substantive changes to key actions; key action added; ordering changes
	• Applying Innovation	New
Interpersonal Competencies	Interpersonal Skills	Name change
• Building trust	• Building trust	No change
• Communicating effectively	• Communicating effectively	No change
• Influencing stakeholders	• Influencing stakeholders	No change
• Leveraging diversity		Incorporated into "Global Mindset"
• Networking and partnering	• Networking and partnering	Minor changes to key actions
	• Emotional intelligence	New
Personal Competencies	Personal Skills	Name change
• Demonstrating adaptability	• Demonstrating adaptability	No change
• Modeling personal development	• Modeling personal development	One key action removed ("maintains professional knowledge") and moved to Industry Knowledge
	Industry Knowledge	New
	Technology Literacy	New
	Global Mindset	New

Delivering Training (now Training Delivery) as well as new content on informal learning methods, social media, and leveraging technology. Measurement and Evaluation (now Evaluating Learning Impact) incorporates learning analytics. Managing Organizational Knowledge (now Knowledge Management) no longer incudes activities typically carried out by information technology. Career Planning and Talent Management (now Integrated Talent Management) better reflects integrated talent management activities.

Table 3.3: Changes to the Areas of Expertise

Original Name (2004)	New Name (2013)	Extent of Content Changes	Description of Content Changes
Designing Learning	Instructional Design	Substantial	Name change; addition of mobile learning, social learning, informal learning approaches
Delivering Training	Training Delivery	Substantial	Name change; changes to statements (see Designing Learning)
Human Performance Improvement	Performance Improvement	Minor	Name change; minor updates
Measuring and Evaluating	Evaluating Learning Impact	Substantial	Name change; holistic change to focus on learning analytics; substantial updates to statements
Managing the Learning Function	Managing Learning Programs	Minor	Name change; minor updates
Managing Organizational Knowledge*	Knowledge Management	Substantial	Name change; substantial changes to statements include the elimination of statements and increased emphasis on informal learning approaches
Career Planning and Talent Management	Integrated Talent Management	Substantial	Name change; holistic change to focus less on career planning and more on talent management as an integrated system and knowing how learning fits into it
Coaching	Coaching	Minor	Minor updates
Facilitating Organizational Change	Change Management	Minor	Name change; minor updates
	Learning Technologies	New	Added; highlights the importance of T&D professionals applying technology effectively in a training and development context across a number of AOEs

*Managing Organizational Knowledge became Managing Organizational Knowledge/Social Learning in 2011. Social Learning was added in 2011 as a result of a targeted interim update.

Advantages for the Practitioner

If you are already familiar with the previous model, use Tables 3.2 and 3.3 to identify where differences exist and where you will need to update your knowledge. Content that is either new or significantly changed should be reviewed carefully. In the Foundational Competencies, pay particular attention to the additions of Industry Knowledge, Technology Literacy, Global Mindset, and innovation (under Business Skills). These competencies and characteristics are emphasized in the 2013 Model because of their growing importance. More specifically, Industry Knowledge addresses the need for development professionals to know the latest practices and to have the business- or sector-specific knowledge they need for their operating environment.

To stay relevant and effective in today's dynamic organizations, training and development professionals need to maintain a sharp focus on what competencies are important and develop a strategy to acquire them.

It is important to note that the Model is both broad and deep. **The extent to which each individual needs to master the various competencies depends on a person's current role and future aspirations.** For example, specialists and experts may wish to focus their development energy on mastering one or two of the AOEs. Business managers or leaders may wish to spend more time mastering a broad array of Foundational Competencies and ensuring they have exposure across all the AOEs. All training professionals need to know a bit of everything in the Model, but the extent to which they need to focus and dive deep will vary by individual and the relevance of the competencies to the business in which they operate.

Call to Action

The ASTD 2013 Competency Model urges training and development professionals and their organizations to keep their skills current. In general terms, practitioners are advised to:

- update their knowledge of new and emerging technologies and how they apply to the training and development profession
- deepen their understanding of data and how to apply them, especially in the context of Evaluating Learning Impact and Integrated Talent Management

- continue to deepen understanding of key Foundational Competencies, including Industry Knowledge, Global Mindset, Technology Literacy, and innovation
- continue to align training and development efforts with business goals and use business metrics to demonstrate training's contribution to organizational success.

For step-by-step guidance on how to use the ASTD Competency Model for individual professional development, see chapter 4.

CHAPTER 4

Applying the ASTD Competency Model

The ASTD Competency Model was meticulously researched and validated. This chapter looks at practical applications of the Model.

The Foundational Competencies and AOEs defined in this report pinpoint the knowledge, skills, abilities and behaviors that are critical for training and development professionals. However, the real value of the Model is realized in its application.

Integrated HR Systems

Training and development professionals need to work within their organizations to incorporate the Foundational Competencies and AOEs into their own human resource (HR) systems to:

- attract talent
- evaluate individuals for selection and promotion
- inform training and development programs
- guide career planning decisions
- assess job performance
- inform coaching and feedback
- establish internal certification programs.

Figure 4.1 depicts the various HR systems that can be built around competencies. Various HR systems can create one integrated system by relating each to a common set of competencies. Because the same competencies and AOEs underpin all of the systems, each part operates more efficiently. In turn, training costs decrease due to the benefits of having a common competency framework and language.

Figure 4.1: Integrated HR Systems

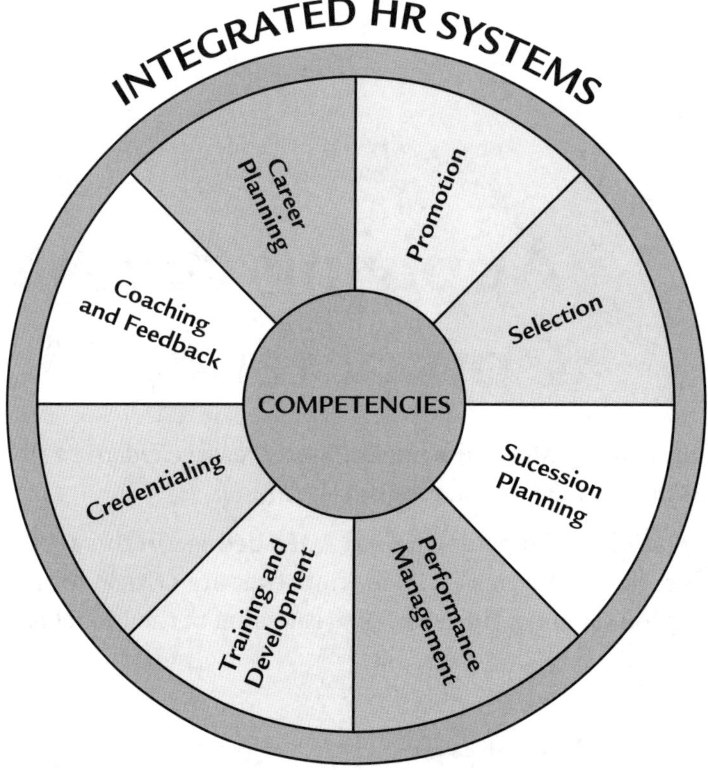

How Leaders Can Use the Model

For chief learning officers (CLOs) and other training and development managers, the ASTD Competency Model can serve as a template for success today and in the future. The Model may be used to determine which competencies and AOEs are appropriate for a unit's training and development professionals. Leaders need to integrate these competencies and AOEs into their HR systems so that these standards and expectations become ingrained and incentivized in their organizations.

Leaders and managers in the profession must demand excellence from their staff—whether they are internal resources or external vendors or partners. This means that leaders and managers must challenge their training professionals to effectively demonstrate all the competencies needed for their areas of responsibility. Leaders also are responsible for ensuring that practitioners are competent and held in regard by business leaders. One way to do this is to encourage professionals to expand and enhance their skills. See appendix F for a job aid to help leaders use the ASTD Competency Model for professional development and workforce planning purposes for their organizations.

How Organizations Can Use the Model

With the help of individual leaders and managers, organizations can use the ASTD Competency Model to improve performance in a number of ways, such as:

- **Performance management:** The Model provides excellent content that can be used in a comprehensive or upgraded performance management program. Regardless of the type of assessment being developed, the Model provides the foundation and specific language for these activities.
- **Strategy alignment:** A common theme throughout the ASTD Competency Model is the importance of connecting training and development activities to the organization. The Model is an excellent resource to help build a scorecard to ensure that the training and development function meets the strategic and operational needs of the business and that the right skills are in place both now and in the future to accomplish the mission.
- **Benchmarking:** Because the Model reflects current and emerging practices across the industry, learning leaders and managers can use it to build a comprehensive benchmarking tool to ensure that resources are used and managed effectively.
- **Managing talent:** The ASTD Competency Model provides a comprehensive road map and is an appropriate tool to help leaders manage the talent in their training function. Organizations using the Model for this purpose are able to develop comprehensive assessment tools for both selection and development purposes.

How Individual Contributors Can Use the Model

"Am I performing effectively today, and am I ready for the future?" is the question that every professional should be asking. One of the most direct ways to answer this question is to assess current performance against the competencies. The ASTD Competency Model clearly describes what competencies professionals should have today and in the future.

First, the ASTD Competency Model shows how all components of the profession relate to each other and allows training and development professionals to see how their jobs fit into the broader range of competencies across the profession.

Second, professionals can drill into the key knowledge and action details (in appendixes D and E) for the purpose of targeting skill development. The Model offers several distinct ways for individuals to approach this:

- **Development:** Each of the 10 Areas of Expertise (AOEs) offers concrete guidance for self-development by linking successful performance to specific actions and behaviors. Once skills gaps have been identified, professionals can work with their managers or other experts to build the skills and behaviors required for career advancement. See appendix G for a self-assessment tool to help individuals use the ASTD Competency Model for professional development purposes. Most notably, it is designed to help individuals identify and create an action plan to close skills gaps.
- **Career exploration:** Most respondents to Competency Model research surveys reported that they spend their careers working across several different AOEs. The Model is a broad map of career possibilities in many professional roles and the skills and abilities needed for such roles. Contributors in various roles can use the Model as it pertains to career development as follows:
    - ***Learning executive:*** Professionals at the highest level of the field may need broad awareness of all 10 AOEs to ensure they can lead the function well and also so that there are no critical gaps in bench strength. For example, if a company emphasizes the effective and innovative use of technology to deliver training, but has given little or no consideration to evaluating learning impact, then having this knowledge might urge the CLO to place more emphasis on addressing this key deficit area.
    - ***External consultant:*** While the key Foundational Competencies of external consultants may include analyzing needs, proposing solutions, networking, and partnering, the depth of functional expertise these professionals bring to their jobs can vary greatly. It may be necessary for consultants to be familiar with all 10 AOEs to stay relevant and well-rounded.

- ***Subject matter expert (SME):*** SMEs and other content experts may have deep subject matter expertise in certain topics and subjects. But often they have virtually no formal education around how to instruct when they are tapped to train others. These individuals can benefit from a review of the ASTD Competency Model—especially the areas of Instructional Design and Training Delivery—to help them become better facilitators. For example, a SME with a long history of teaching on a specific topic may discover that a current program does not apply adult learning principles, and therefore may decide to improve the design and delivery of the instructional program.

How Educators Can Use the Model

Many organizations and learning institutions—including colleges, universities, business schools, and professional associations—are committed to advancing the training and development profession by developing practitioners in the field. The competency and AOE definitions plus the key actions serve as excellent tools for evaluating current curricula and planning new offerings. The ASTD Competency Model also provides the focal point for prioritizing lifelong learning. Educators can use the Model to:

- assess learners' needs by measuring current skills against the competencies and AOEs
- take stock of learners' interest in enhancing their development
- evaluate existing course offerings to see which aspects of the Model they need to address
- update existing course offerings to include broader coverage of AOEs and competencies
- plan an entire curriculum for the profession
- develop specific course offerings to improve performance in particular areas
- guide student development paths by evaluating individual development needs
- create tests and measures to evaluate performance in the competencies and AOEs
- evaluate and build faculty expertise.

By following the recommendations in this chapter, training and development professionals can maximize the benefit of using the 2013 ASTD Competency Model.

CHAPTER 5

Questions and Answers

Chapters 1-4 explained the new ASTD Competency Model and its value to practitioners at all levels, to organizations, and to the training and development profession. This chapter answers the following questions:

1. Can the ASTD Competency Model be used in any organizational culture? Is one type of culture better suited to its use than another?
2. Is the Competency Model useful for all types of training practitioners?
3. Does the Competency Model describe different levels of proficiency within a competency?
4. Are any self-evaluation tools provided for those who wish to benchmark their current competencies against those of the new Competency Model?
5. How can subject matter experts use the Model?
6. What are the first steps individual practitioners should take to align their current competencies with those of the new Model?
7. How can academics use the new Competency Model?
8. How might training staff leaders use the Model?
9. What's the best way to tailor the Competency Model to my organization?
10. What is the expected shelf life of the skills and abilities described in the Competency Model?
11. When does ASTD expect to update the 2013 version of the Competency Model?

1. Can the ASTD Competency Model be used in any organizational culture? Is one type of culture better suited to its use than another?

The ASTD Competency Model is not organization specific or nation specific. While the competencies it describes may be universal, the measurement of behaviors associated with them will vary. The ASTD 2013 Competency Study is primarily based on data from North America. While some international data were collected, the Model must be tailored to fit specific national and cultural norms and differences.

2. Is the Competency Model useful for all types of training practitioners?

The training and development field includes many individuals with different goals and aspirations. To illustrate:

- Some enter the field and remain in it for their entire careers as internal practitioners or external consultants.
- Some rotate through the training and development function to build expertise, technical knowledge, and visibility as they advance through an organization.
- Some line (operating) managers may have training and development responsibilities but may not be aware of them or feel equipped to carry them out.
- In small organizations, competence may be required in all areas of the field, whereas in large organizations, practitioners may specialize in just one or two.

The ASTD Competency Study is intended to be broadly applicable across the entire training and development profession but not targeted to a particular group or role. Thus, its use requires judgment in its application and tailoring to suit the specific needs of the user.

3. Does the Competency Model describe different levels of proficiency within a competency?

The simple answer is no. Further work would be needed to identify different levels of proficiency for behaviors tied to the competencies. See the sidebar for a few resources on developing behaviorally anchored rating scales (BARS).

How to Develop Behaviorally Anchored Rating Scales (BARS): A Reference List

Here are a few resources to help you develop behaviorally anchored ratings scales:

Bernardin, H.J. (2002). *Human Resource Management: An Experiential Approach.* 3rd ed. New York: McGraw-Hill.

Johnson, J.M., & H.S. Pennypacker. (2008). *Strategies and Tactics of Behavioral Research.* 3rd ed. London: Routledge.

Kingstrom, P.O., & A.R. Bass. (1981). A Critical Analysis of Studies Comparing Behaviorally Anchored Ratings Scales (BARS) and Other Rating Formats. *Personnel Psychology,* 34, 263–289.

Landy, F.J., & J.M. Conte. (2009). *Work in the 21st Century: An Introduction to Industrial and Organizational Psychology.* 3rd ed. San Francisco: Wiley-Blackwell.

Lloyd, K. Behind BARS: Evaluating Employees with Behaviorally Anchored Rating Scales. www.dummies.com/how-to/content/behind-bars-evaluating-employees-with-behaviorally.html

Schwab, D.P., H.G. Heneman, & T.A. Decotiis. (1975). Behaviorally Anchored Rating Scales: A Review of the Literature. *Personnel Psychology,* 28, 549–562.

4. Are any self-evaluation tools provided for those who wish to benchmark their current competencies against those of the new Competency Model?

ASTD continually develops new content that aligns to the Model and tools to make the competencies more actionable. For the most up-to-date content, visit www.astd.org/model and the ASTD Career Navigator at www.astd.org/careernavigator as referenced in the sidebar, "More Tools and Resources."

More Tools and Resources

To Find	Go To	Details
An online assessment to help you or your team to develop an employee or career development action plan	The Career Navigator™	www.astd.org/careernavigator
The complete 2004 Study: Mapping the Future	www.astd.org	http://store.astd.org Product Code: 110407
More information and job aids	The ASTD website	www.astd.org/model

5. How can subject matter experts use the Model?

The ASTD Competency Model describes the competencies essential for high-performing training and development experts. However, it can also be a useful tool to help subject matter experts (SMEs) become better at instructional design and facilitation techniques.

6. What are the first steps individual practitioners should take to align their current competencies with those of the new Model?

Start with personal strengths, areas for improvement, and your career goals. Do some soul-searching and seek input from those who know your professional strengths and weaknesses.

Use the Areas of Expertise (AOEs) to decide which areas to work in. If you don't know, try volunteering your time to try out areas you are thinking about.

Another option is to participate in industry conferences where you will meet people with insights about how to take the next steps in your professional development and career journey.

Once you know what you want to do and what you are good at, consider whether to be a generalist or a specialist. If you choose to be a generalist, try to learn about as many AOEs as possible. If you choose to be a specialist, you may wish to enroll in courses related to the AOEs in which you want to specialize.

Find mentors who are in the jobs you aspire to and formulate questions for them. As you gain experience and education, you will become an increasingly sophisticated user of the Model to build your expertise.

Later on, you may also wish to acquire a professional certification, such as ASTD Certification Institute's CPLP (Certified Professional in Learning and Performance). Visit www.astd.org/cplp for more details.

7. How can academics use the new Competency Model?

There are at least two ways for instructors or professors to use the Model. One way is to use it as a reference tool for students enrolled in training and development courses. Instructors can share the Model and ask students to review the sections that they think apply to them. The Model is an excellent starting point to discuss a student's career choices.

The second way is for academics to use the ASTD Competency Model as a foundation for academic curricula for the field. The AOEs may reflect planned courses. Groups of competencies within an AOE may be grouped together as courses.

8. How might training staff leaders use the Model?

Training staff leaders can use the Model for career and developmental discussions with training and development practitioners. With some work, the Model can become the foundation of a culture-specific competency model for a team or organization.

9. What's the best way to tailor the Competency Model to my organization?

To tailor the Model to your team or organization, consider hiring a competency model expert. For tools on how to adapt the Model to meet your organizational needs and requirements, see the sidebar, "How to Customize Competency Models" (for a reference list) and appendix H.

How to Customize Competency Models: A Reference List

Here are a few resources to help with tailoring the Model:

Caruso, K. (2011, May 12). Competency Models: One Size Does Not Fit All. See: http://web.viapeople.com/viaPeople-blog/bid/53355/Competency-Models-One-Size-Does-Not-Fit-All

Gupta, S.R. (2007). *A Quick Guide to Cultural Competency.* Anaheim, CA: Gupta Consulting Group.

Rothwell, W., & J. Graber. (2010). *Competency-Based Training Basics.* Alexandria, VA: ASTD.

Rothwell, W., J. Graber, & D. Dubois. (2013, in press). *The Competency Toolkit.* 2 vols. 2nd ed. Amherst, MA: HRD Press.

Sanghi, S. (2007). *The Handbook of Competency Mapping: Understanding, Designing, and Implementing Competency Models in Organizations.* 2nd ed. Thousand Oaks, CA: Sage.

10. What is the expected shelf life of the skills and abilities described in the Competency Model?

In today's rapidly changing business environment, the shelf life of professional knowledge and skills can be short. The Competency Model can be used to assess one's current skills and to look into the future. Training and development managers can use the Model to facilitate discussions with individuals and entire staffs about competencies needed today and in the future. Typically, competency models have a shelf life of five to seven years before substantial revisions are required.

11. When does ASTD expect to update the 2013 version of the Competency Model?

The Competency Model is the foundation for content from ASTD. It forms the basis of ASTD's educational offerings and the ASTD Certification Institute's CPLP certification program.

ASTD is committed to providing the most up-to-date information to its members and the profession it serves. Look for minor updates every few years and major updates every five to seven years in keeping with industry best practices.

CHAPTER 6

Examples of the Proven Value of the ASTD Competency Model

If the cliché "the proof of the pudding is in the eating" carries any weight, then individuals, organizations, education institutions, and the training and development profession will find plenty of real value to extract from the 2013 ASTD Competency Model.

The benefits to professionals are self-evident in the Model-aligned Certified Professional in Learning and Performance (CPLP) certification program, judging from the growing number of training and development professionals currently earning their CPLP certifications.

Forward-looking organizations have also discovered the Model's value and are aligning the knowledge, skills, abilities, and behaviors of their training and development staff to current professional practices while preparing to meet future ones. Other organizations are using the Model to build comprehensive performance management systems for their organizations.

Individual contributors and practitioners, especially those in leadership positions, increasingly rely on the Model as a well-researched tool to help them identify the specific skills they need to advance their and their staff's careers.

For those who teach and plan curricula for training and development professionals, the ASTD Competency Model has proven itself a valuable classroom tool and a foundation on which to build academic curricula.

While these benefits are certainly true, nothing validates real-world application like examples from the field. What follows are a few examples that clearly demonstrate the previous Model's value to four organizations: the University System of Georgia, ASTD's Metro DC Chapter, Hilton Worldwide, and ASTD's San Diego Chapter.

University System of Georgia

The University System of Georgia's Board of Regents recognized the need for developing HR leadership at the system level in 2009 after a close examination of its 35 academic institutions.

At the time, each of these institutions had its own HR department and each institution's level of training and development capacity varied. Some programs were well established, while others had limited personnel and resources dedicated to training and development.

Faced with this challenge, Tina Woodard, Assistant Vice Chancellor for Organizational Development in the Board of Regents' office, launched the Professional Development Consortium (PDC; for more information on the PDC, see http://www.usg.edu/hr/development/professional_development_consortium). Consisting of HR and OD staff from six key institutions within the University System of Georgia, the PDC leveraged the existing training and development capacity of these key institutions to create Regional Training Centers responsible for (a) conducting training needs assessments for institutions in its region, (b) developing training programs, and (c) sharing resources.

The mission of the PDC is to facilitate collaboration and organizational learning with a central goal of increasing the training and development capacity between HR and OD professionals at each institution.

The ASTD Competency Model and other ASTD products played a key role in accomplishing these objectives. The system used the ASTD Competency Model as the basis for conducting system wide, regional, and institutional needs assessments. For example, through surveys and qualitative discussions, the Competency Model was used to identify gaps in training and development knowledge and skills among the HR and OD staff.

PDC staff created a core set of system wide training courses for professionals in the university system using the results of these needs assessments. The PDC also conducted train-the-trainer sessions with institutions that had fewer than average established training and development personnel to ensure these programs were administered effectively. Individual institutions and the university system also purchased a number of ASTD publications such as *Infoline*, the ASTD Learning System, ASTD Press books, and *T+D* to help build training and development capacity.

To further deepen training and development capacity, the university system assembled a virtual study group to prepare HR and OD professionals within the system to obtain a Certified Professional in Learning and Performance (CPLP) designation. However, the goal of this effort is not solely to obtain credentials, but also to build training and development skills among employees and increase community among individuals doing training and development work. Study group participants and facilitators are also using ASTD's preparation resources (for example, the CPLP Study Group Leader's Guide) to meet these objectives.

In short, the University System of Georgia uses the Competency Model to identify the competencies needed to perform training and development work and then uses ASTD products to help increase its HR and OD employees' collective skill set.

ASTD's Metro DC Chapter

ASTD's Metro DC Chapter takes full advantage of ASTD's Competency Model and uses it as a key strategic and organizational guide for the 350+ member chapter that includes the District of Columbia and portions of Virginia and Maryland.

According to former Chapter President Michelle Moore, the first benefit of the Model is that it provides the Metro DC Chapter members with a common language to discuss the training and development field. She said the Model also provides organizational focus as well as a strategic framework to discuss the overall direction of the Metro DC Chapter. She noted that this benefit is especially appreciated during chapter board meetings when the language of the Model helps keep everyone on the same page when critical discussions occur.

Program development at the Metro DC Chapter is also tied to the Model. The chapter organizes a variety of evening and daylong workshops for its members and all use specific components of the Competency Model as the basis for the learning events. Moore noted that by using the Model she is able to ensure that members' needs are met and no important developments in the training field are overlooked.

The Competency Model also plays a key role in the chapter's career development and sponsorships and in internal professional development operations. Moore noted that during her tenure as president, the Competency Model was her go-to document when members approached her with questions about career development. She said that the Model allowed her to discuss very specific aspects of a member's career and to make concrete recommendations that she could link directly to information in the ASTD Certification Institute's Candidate Bulletin.

Sponsoring organizations also benefited from the use of the Competency Model, Moore said, because it allowed chapter leadership to address specifically how their sponsorship supports the training and development field.

Clearly, the Competency Model is an important operational tool that provides a wide range of benefits for the Metro DC Chapter. Other ASTD chapters should consider the use of the Competency Model and the potential it offers to improve key stakeholders' service and support.

Hilton Worldwide

Hilton Worldwide uses the ASTD Competency Model in at least three specific ways to support its strong commitment to the continued growth and development of its global workforce and to ensure that all its training and development professionals have the right competencies for success.

First, Hilton uses the Model along with an established enterprise wide general competency model to provide a lens for assessing the technical skills and the job knowledge of employees during annual and midyear reviews and to zero in on areas for improvement. Team members and their managers also use ASTD's Career Navigator—a tool designed to help individuals and their managers assess and identify needed current and future knowledge and skills—as part of this standard assessment protocol.

Second, Hilton supports the Competency Model through its support of CPLP certification; nearly every member of its curriculum design team has the CPLP designation. Hilton's consistent support of the Model is rooted in the belief that the Competency Model defines the field for practitioners, provides a common language for better communication, and sets a solid competency baseline for all team members.

Third, the Model's clearly defined set of broad and specific competencies provides a neutral basis to examine individual team members' and the organization's strengths and weaknesses. This knowledge then helps identify gaps that need attention.

Hilton's use of ASTD's Competency Model is a concrete example of how leading-edge organizations can use and adapt the Model in ways that provide real individual and organizational value while offering clear pathways for positive career and organizational improvement.

ASTD's San Diego Chapter

Former ASTD San Diego Chapter President, Phillip Tanzilo, says his experience in 2006 of using the ASTD Competency Model to turn around the once-struggling chapter is a good example of the Model's transformational power.

Not only did the Competency Model drive the chapter's renewed strategic planning efforts that year, it also served as a standard tool to assist with career and personal development advice, and was the basis for all of the chapter's marketing and programming decisions. The coordinated effort, Tanzilo says, achieved some remarkable results.

According to Tanzilo, when he took over as chapter president in 2006 during an economic downturn with high local unemployment, membership was falling and finances were in the red. He and the other 14 board members were looking for some guidance to turn the fortunes of the chapter around. When he and the board discovered the ASTD Competency Model, they all knew they had struck gold.

Tanzilo said the Model was the perfect supporting tool for the 2006 strategic planning theme, "Fresh, Focused, and Aligned," and as it turned out, the Model became the basis for the most important chapter functions, operations, and mission directions, including chapter leadership.

The ASTD Competency Model served as a valuable and comprehensive career and personal development road map. Tanzilo says that this core value was quickly realized among chapter members as new programs were rolled out that directly aligned to the Model.

The board also saw value in the Model as a tool to provide consistency to the job of board member. Prior to the Model's introduction, the chapter had a difficult time transitioning new board members to service. It was also difficult to find the right individuals to serve in the vacant slots created by departing members. The ASTD Competency Model was the natural benchmark for board members to use when they created their own Board Leadership Competency Model, designed specifically to ensure that each board slot is filled with the right individual who has the key values, knowledge, skills, and abilities to do the job.

In addition, the San Diego Chapter used the nine Areas of Expertise (AOEs) in the 2004 ASTD Competency Model as the basis for marketing its professional development programs. This alignment provided a much-needed message about the value of membership to new and potential members. Monthly chapter meetings also featured speakers aligned to the Model, as did the chapter newsletter, *Training Trends*. Even the chapter's first annual conference in 2006, *Your Turn to Learn*, aligned its learning tracks to the AOEs in the Competency Model.

The efforts paid off for the chapter both in internal chapter operations and external results. The consistency that the Model brought to board leadership resulted in greater engagement. All 14 volunteer board members were retained that year in clearly defined roles. Membership increased that year from 390 to over 500 members, and the chapter finances improved from being in the red to having a cash reserve. Clearly, use of the Model was a real win for the ASTD San Diego Chapter.

The 2013 ASTD Competency Model was developed with the input of hundreds of thought leaders, experts, and training and development practitioners. It provides a common language and framework of competencies that define the current and future states of the training and development profession.

The Model redefines training and development competencies in light of profound changes in technology, the economy, and new expectations that organizations have about the contribution of employee training to their success. As such, it is a blueprint for success for training and development professionals, for organizations, for educational institutions, and for the profession.

Prior ASTD Competency Studies and Key Findings

Study	Description	Key Findings
2004: *ASTD Competency Study: Mapping the Future*	More than 2,000 training and development professionals and senior leaders from around the world participated in the *ASTD Competency Study: Mapping the Future*. The principle objectives were to: 1) identify the most significant trends and drivers that would impact current and future practice; 2) describe a comprehensive, inspiring, and future-oriented competency model; and 3) provide a foundation for competency-based applications, deliverables, and outputs—including certification.	The Study identified eight key trends for which training and development professionals should prepare, including: 1. Drastic times, drastic measures 2. Blurred lines—life or work 3. Small world and shrinking 4. New faces, new expectations 5. Work be nimble, work be quick 6. Security alert! 7. Life and work in the e-lane 8. A higher ethical bar The Study identified three major categories (clusters) of Foundational Competencies and four key roles associated with each category—intrapersonal, business/management, and personal—and nine major Areas of Expertise (AOEs) needed by training and development professionals: 1. Designing Training 2. Improving Human Performance 3. Delivering Training 4. Measuring and Evaluating 5. Facilitating Organizational Change 6. Managing the Learning Function 7. Coaching 8. Managing Organizational Knowledge 9. Career Planning and Talent Management

Study	Description	Key Findings
1999: *ASTD Models for Workplace Learning and Performance*	Practitioners, senior practitioners, and line managers provided input for the *ASTD Models for Workplace Learning and Performance* to determine what current and future competencies (five years beyond 1999) would be required to succeed in the field. The 1999 report defined workplace learning and performance as "the integrated use of learning and other interventions for the purpose of improving individual and organizational performance."	This report defined roles (not job titles) as "a grouping of competencies targeted to meet specific expectations of a job or function." (Rothwell, et al., 1999, xv). Seven workplace learning and performance roles were identified, including manager, analyst, intervention selector, intervention designer, intervention implementor, change leader, and evaluator. A set of 52 specific competencies were identified, classified into six groups: 1. ***Analytical Competencies***—the creation of new understandings or methods through the synthesis of multiple ideas, processes, and data 2. ***Technical Competencies***—the understanding and application of existing knowledge or processes 3. ***Leadership Competencies***—influencing, enabling, or inspiring others to act 4. ***Business Competencies***—understanding organizations as systems and the processes, decision criteria, and issues that businesses face 5. ***Interpersonal Competencies***—understanding and applying methods that produce effective interactions between people and groups 6. ***Technological Competencies***—understanding and applying current, new, or emerging technologies
1998: *ASTD Models for Learning Technologies*	*ASTD Models for Learning Technologies* examined the roles, competencies, and work outputs that Human Resource Development (HRD) professionals need in order to implement learning technologies in their organizations. HRD professionals were identified as those who use training and development, organization development, and career development to improve individual, group, and organizational effectiveness.	The 1998 Study provided a classification system that related instructional methods (for example, lectures, role plays, and simulations) to presentation methods (for example, computer-based training, electronic performance support systems, multimedia, and video) and distribution formats (for example, audiotape, CD-ROM, Internet, and videotape; (Piskurich & Sanders, 1998).

Study	Description	Key Findings
1996: *ASTD Models for Human Performance Improvement*	*ASTD Models for Human Performance Improvement* (HPI) explored the roles, competencies, and outputs that human performance improvement professionals (or performance consultants) need in order to effect meaningful change within organizations. The report presented HPI as a process, not a discipline. For example, instructional systems design (ISD) was described as a process used to analyze, design, develop, deliver, and evaluate training programs. Human resource development was described as a discipline meant to carry out the HPI process. Thus, the title *HPI practitioner* represents anyone who solves business problems using the HPI model.	Two key points of the 1996 Study are: • Everyone in organizational settings plays a part in improving performance and contributes to enhanced organizational competitiveness. Practitioners, line managers, employees, and others may perform HPI work; HRD professionals are not its sole practitioners. • No individual plays all the roles or masters all the competencies described in the Study. In addition, the report: • lists trends in five areas: performance, business, learning, organizational structure, and technology • describes 14 terminal outputs of HPI work and 81 enabling outputs. A terminal output is "a final outcome directly associated with a particular role"; an enabling output is "a specific output associated with the demonstration of a particular competency" (p. 79). • pinpoints 15 core and 38 supporting competencies of HPI • summarizes four roles of HPI professionals: analyst, intervention specialist, change manager, and evaluator • identifies 16 key ethical issues affecting HPI work.
1989: *Models for HRD Practice*	*Models for HRD Practice* defined the profession to include career development and organization development as well as training and development. It defined HRD as "the integrated use of training and development, organization development, and career development to improve individual, group, and organizational effectiveness."	The 1989 Study depicted HRD within the larger human resource field as a wheel encompassing activities including training and development, organization development, career development, organization/job design, human resource planning, performance management systems, selection and staffing, compensation and benefits, employee assistance, union/labor relations, human resource research, and information systems. In addition, the Study: • described 74 outputs of HRD work and identified quality requirements for each output • pinpointed 35 competencies for HRD and identified key ethical issues affecting HRD • summarized 11 HRD roles, including researcher, marketer, organization change agent, needs analyst, program designer, HRD materials developer, instructor/facilitator, individual career development advisor, administrator, evaluator, and HRD manager.

Study	Description	Key Findings
1983: *Models for Excellence*	*Models for Excellence* defined training and development and established the format for all the ASTD Competency Model studies published since 1983.	*Models for Excellence* was launched in 1981 when Patricia McLagan carried out a series of studies focused on training and development and the trainer's role. The 1983 report (McLagan & McCullough, 1983) included: • a depiction of HRD as a wheel • a definition of training and development • a list of 34 forces expected to affect the T&D field • 15 T&D roles • 102 critical outputs for the T&D field • 31 T&D competencies • four role clusters • a matrix of 15 roles/31 competencies.
1978: *A Study of Professional Training and Development Roles and Competencies*	*A Study of Professional Training and Development Roles and Competencies* defined the basic skills, knowledge, and other attributes required for effective performance of training and development activities. The Study questioned more than 14,000 ASTD members in the United States, Canada, and Mexico, and 500 members outside North America.	The 1978 Study, conducted by Patrick Pinto and James Walker, revealed the following major areas for T&D practitioners: • analyzing and diagnosing needs • determining appropriate training approaches • designing and developing programs • developing material resources • managing internal resources • managing external resources • developing and counseling individuals • preparing job- or performance-related training • conducting classroom training • developing group and organization development • conducting research on training • managing working relationships with managers and clients • managing the training and development function • managing professional self-development.

APPENDIX B

Data Collection Details

Introduction

The 2013 ASTD Competency Study is a rigorous evaluation of the 2004 Competency Study research, with a particular focus on the Areas of Expertise (AOEs). Several sources of data were used to inform decisions about how to revise the 2004 Model, including:

- existing data from ASTD, such as Certified Performance and Learning Professional (CPLP) exam item statistics, CPLP exam feedback, perspectives of key stakeholders, and ASTD research reports
- interviews and focus groups with a cross section of subject matter experts (SMEs)
- surveys of the profession (both targeted and large-scale surveys of training and development professionals who are ASTD members or are otherwise associated with ASTD).

Review of the ASTD Data

After conducting a thorough literature review, the research team conducted interviews with key stakeholders. The purpose of these interviews was fourfold: 1) to gather perspectives on the 2004 ASTD Competency Model in general, and the Areas of Expertise (AOEs) in particular; 2) to collect feedback about any issues or concerns with the Model; 3) to identify trends and developments in the field that may affect the 2004 Competency Model; and 4) to gather perceptions regarding the products associated with the Model. All interviewees have had significant exposure to the 2004 ASTD Competency Model and associated products. The researchers analyzed the content of interview responses and identified common themes.

The research team gathered additional data from subject matter experts associated with the CPLP certification work product scoring process. These subject matter experts had in-depth knowledge of the ASTD Competency Model and respective AOEs.

The researchers conducted three independent surveys focusing on the relevance and importance of the AOEs. The first two were conducted in the early phase of the Study to get a sense for how relevant the existing content was for the field (these are referred to as "marketplace pulse check surveys"). The third was a large-scale survey conducted at the end of the project with training and development professionals who were primarily ASTD national members.

Competency Survey

The first of the two pulse check surveys focused explicitly on the importance of the AOEs, their knowledge and action components, and the roles in the Competency Model. This survey is referred to as the "competency survey." The target audience for this survey included individuals who know the industry well because of their levels of experience and exposure to the field. This included CPLP credential holders, ASTD chapter leaders, and higher education thought leaders. Contact information for the target audience was gathered from ASTD records. In total, 188 (8.67 percent) respondents fully completed the survey. This response rate is in line with that of the original (2004) survey, which had a response rate of 5.9 percent.

Approximately 78 percent of competency survey respondents were age 40 or over (see Table 1), 62 percent of the sample had a master's degree or higher (Table 2), and 94 percent of respondents had over five years of experience in the field (Table 3). Furthermore, respondents tended to have advanced skill levels and career roles (Table 4). Taken together, these data indicate that the people in the sample were equipped to make judgments about those competencies required for success in the training and development profession.

Table 1. Age Distribution of Survey Respondents

Age	Frequency	Percent
29 or less	5	2.7
30 to 39	34	18.7
40 to 49	63	34.6
50 to 59	60	33.0
60 or over	20	11.0
Total	182	100

Table 2. Highest Level of Education Achieved

Educational Background	Frequency	Percent
Some Trade/Business School Training	1	0.5
Some University/College Education	8	4.4
University/College Graduate	39	21.4
Some Post-Graduate Education	21	11.5
Master's Degree	98	53.8
Advanced Graduate or Professional Degree	15	8.2
Total	182	100

Table 3. Years of Experience in the Training and Development Profession

Years of Experience	Frequency	Percent
1 to 2 years	1	0.5
3 to 5 years	10	5.5
6 to 10 years	42	23.1
11 to 15 years	43	23.6
16 to 20 years	39	21.4
More than 20 years	47	25.8
Total	182	100

Table 4. Career Role and Skill Level

Career Role and Skill Level	Frequency	Percent
Entry-Level	1	0.5
Mid-Level Specialist	24	13.1
Senior-Level Specialist	63	34.4
Entry-Level Manager	7	3.8
Mid-Level Manager	41	22.4
Senior-Level Manager	20	10.9
Entry- to Mid-Level Executive	11	6.0
Mid- to Senior-Level Executive	16	8.7
Total	183	100

As indicated by Tables 5 and 6, the sample represented a broad cross section of the training and development profession in terms of area of responsibility and industry.

Table 5. Major Area of Responsibility

Responsibility	Frequency	Percent
Training Delivery	33	18.2
Instructional Design	52	28.7
Career Development	4	2.2
Coaching	2	1.1
Leadership Development, Management Development, & Executive Development	17	9.4
Performance Consulting	21	11.6
Change Management, Organization Development, Organizational Effectiveness	26	14.4
Knowledge Management	1	0.6
Measurement and Evaluation	2	1.1
Human Capital/Talent Management	13	7.2
Educational Technology	3	1.7
Human Resource Management	4	2.2
Other Specific Human Resource Responsibility	3	1.7
Total	181	100

Table 6. Industry of Respondent

Industry	Frequency	Percent
Agriculture, Forestry, Fishing, and Hunting	1	0.6
Arts, Entertainment, and Recreation	6	3.3
Broadcasting and Communications	3	1.7
Business Schools and Computer Management Training	1	0.6
Colleges, Universities, and Professional Schools	19	10.5
Finance and Insurance	30	16.6
Healthcare and Social Assistance	20	11.0
Information (other services)	1	0.6
Management Consulting Services (including HRD consulting)	17	9.4
Manufacturing	15	8.3
National Security	3	1.7
Public Administration (including government)	10	5.5
Real Estate and Rental and Leasing	3	1.7
Retail Trade	7	3.9
Software Publishing	4	2.2
Transportation and Warehousing	5	2.8
Utilities	2	1.1
Wholesale Trade	34	18.8
Total	181	100

Table 7 shows those AOEs in which respondents had the greatest (self-selected) expertise. As expected, the majority of respondents indicated primary expertise in Delivering Training and Designing Learning; however, all nine AOEs identified in the 2004 Competency Study were represented in the sample.

Table 7. Professional/Technical Competencies of Primary Expertise

Area of Expertise	Frequency	Percent
Career Planning and Talent Management	6	2.9
Coaching	8	3.9
Delivering Training	60	29.0
Designing Learning	70	33.8
Facilitating Organizational Change	19	9.2
Improving Human Performance	14	6.8
Managing Organizational Knowledge	1	0.5
Managing the Learning Function	26	12.6
Measuring and Evaluating	3	1.4
Total	207	100

Table 8 shows respondents' affiliation with ASTD.

Table 8. ASTD Affiliation

Affiliation	Frequency	Percent
ASTD National Member	172	94.0
ASTD Chapter Leader	66	36.1
ASTD Chapter Member	129	70.5
Higher Education Faculty/Staff	25	13.7
CPLP Credential Holder	128	70.0
CPLP Candidate in Progress	3	1.6
Total	183	

Note: Respondents selected all applicable response options.

A critical objective of the current study was to determine whether the importance of the various AOEs has changed in the years subsequent to the 2004 Study. Table 9 shows mean (current) importance ratings by AOE, rank ordered from highest to lowest.

Table 9. Current Importance Ratings by AOE

Area of Expertise	*M*	*SD*
Designing Learning	4.52	0.80
Delivering Training	4.47	0.85
Improving Human Performance	4.07	1.00
Measuring and Evaluating	3.90	1.03
Managing the Learning Function	3.80	1.21
Coaching	3.76	1.11
Facilitating Organizational Change	3.72	1.14
Career Planning and Talent Management	3.52	1.24
Managing Organizational Knowledge	3.46	1.10
Social Learning	3.11	1.18

Note: Ratings were made on a scale from 1 (unnecessary) to 5 (essential).

As indicated in Table 9, all AOEs were considered at least moderately important for successful performance in the profession. However, there was substantial variability in importance ratings across the AOEs. Consistent with the 2004 Study, Designing Learning, Delivering Training, Improving Human Performance, and Measuring and Evaluating were rated as the most important AOEs by the survey respondents. These AOEs also had relatively smaller standard deviations, indicating general agreement from respondents about their importance. Also, similar to the 2004 Study, Managing Organizational Knowledge and Career Planning and Talent Management received relatively lower importance ratings (and had relatively higher lack of agreement). Social Learning received the lowest importance rating in the current study. It was not represented in the 2004 Study.

Respondents were also asked about perceptions of the importance of the different AOEs to successful job performance in the future (the next three years). Table 10 shows these results.

Table 10. Future Importance (Next Three Years) by AOE

Area of Expertise	*M*	*SD*
Designing Learning	4.46	0.87
Improving Human Performance	4.34	0.85
Delivering Training	4.25	0.99
Measuring and Evaluating	4.20	0.93
Facilitating Organizational Change	4.13	1.02
Coaching	3.99	1.04
Managing the Learning Function	3.96	1.10
Managing Organizational Knowledge	3.88	1.00
Career Planning and Talent Management	3.87	1.12
Social Learning	3.78	1.11

These results closely parallel ratings of current importance, in terms of rank ordering of AOEs.

Additionally, respondents had the opportunity to provide importance ratings for the key knowledge and key actions comprising the AOE in which they had the most expertise. All of the key knowledge and actions were rated as at least moderately important. Though small sample sizes preclude drawing strong conclusions from these data, at a minimum, these results suggest that the current list of key knowledge and actions associated with each AOE is generally accurate.

Another goal of the competency survey was to gather perceptions of the appropriateness and importance of the roles in the Competency Model in 2013 and in the next three years (Table 11). All roles were rated as being at least moderately important now and in the future. The role of Learning Strategist was rated as the least important currently, which corresponds to the relatively low ratings of the more strategically oriented AOE of Managing Organizational Knowledge. Ratings of the future importance of the roles showed little differentiation across roles.

Table 11. Current and Future Importance of Roles

Role	*M* (Current)	*SD* (Current)	*M* (Future)	*SD* (Future)
Professional Specialist	4.31	0.93	4.39	0.85
Project Manager	4.00	0.91	4.25	0.85
Business Partner	3.96	1.02	4.47	0.87
Learning Strategist	3.80	1.04	4.43	0.85

The competency survey solicited comments regarding the appropriateness of the roles. In all, 23 respondents provided responses. The majority of comments indicated that the role descriptions are accurate. Additionally, the majority indicated that, in their daily work, they move from role to role on a consistent basis in their organizations. Thus, they cannot be discretely categorized as fitting into one role. These comments suggest that although the roles are relevant, they may not be particularly helpful for characterizing the work of a particular training and development professional.

Additional open-ended questions on the survey asked whether there were AOEs missing in the 2004 Competency Model. The majority of responses to this question did not suggest new AOEs, but instead suggested more specific concepts perceived to be missing from the Model. For example, technology, project management, strategic planning, business impact, return-on-investment (ROI), and financial impacts were all mentioned by multiple respondents as not being sufficiently represented. This was not considered a gap in most cases because the content was already captured in the Model, just not at the top level.

Product Survey

The second pulse check survey was intended to gather information about how well the 2004 Model and its derivative products addressed the needs of employers and practitioners. This is referred to as the "product survey." The product survey included individuals who have used ASTD's competency-based products. This sample was identified through ASTD records and included: a) people who have sent groups of employees through ASTD's Career Navigator, b) individuals who have purchased or used the Career Navigator independently, c) individuals who have purchased the *Mapping the Future* publication since 2007, d) individuals who have purchased the ASTD Learning System and its related products, e) individuals who have purchased ASTD CPLP preparation programs, and f) CPLP On Campus course instructors. The survey was distributed to 5,951 individuals, with 314 providing complete responses, yielding a completion rate of 5.3 percent.

Table 12 shows the age distribution of respondents. The largest percentage of respondents (35 percent) was 40 to 49 years old. The next largest percentage (31 percent) was 50 to 59 years old.

Table 12. Age Distribution

Age	Frequency	Percent
29 or less	13	4.3
30 to 39	72	23.8
40 to 49	105	34.7
50 to 59	94	31.0
60 or over	19	6.3
Total	303	100

The largest percent of responses were from individuals with three to five years of experience (Table 13).

Table 13. Years of Experience in the Training and Development Profession

Years of Experience	Frequency	Percent
None to less than 1 year	11	3.6
1 to 2 years	10	3.3
3 to 5 years	63	20.8
6 to 10 years	59	19.5
11 to 15 years	58	19.1
16 to 20 years	50	16.5
More than 20 years	52	17.2
Total	303	100

The career role breakdown represented a good balance between practitioners and managers (Table 14). The two largest categories of responses were Senior-Level Specialist (22 percent) and Mid-Level Manager (24 percent).

Table 14. Career Role and Skill Level of Respondents

Career Role and Skill Level	Frequency	Percent
Entry-Level	17	5.6
Mid-Level Specialist	63	20.8
Senior-Level Specialist	68	22.4
Entry-Level Manager	10	3.3
Mid-Level Manager	72	23.8
Senior-Level Manager	38	12.5
Entry- to Mid-Level Executive	20	6.6
Mid- to Senior-Level Executive	15	5.0
Total	303	100

Table 15 describes the affiliation of respondents. Respondents could select as many options as applicable.

Table 15. Affiliation with ASTD

Affiliation	Frequency	Percent
ASTD National Member	233	67.1
ASTD Chapter Leader	25	7.2
ASTD Chapter Member	99	28.5
CPLP Credential Holder	37	10.7
CPLP Candidate in Progress	52	15.0
CPLP Prep Class Instructor/Facilitator	4	1.2
Other	19	5.5
Total	469	

Forty-seven percent of the respondents (the largest percentage) reported having a master's degree—indicating a well-educated respondent group (Table 16).

Industries represented by respondents covered the entire spectrum of options, with most respondents reporting Finance and Insurance (18 percent), while Healthcare and Social Assistance (15 percent) made up the second largest category (Table 17).

Table 16. Highest Level of Education Achieved

Educational Background	Frequency	Percent
High School Diploma	1	0.3
Some Trade/Business School Training	7	2.3
Two-Year Degree	7	2.3
Some University/College Education	23	7.6
University/College Graduate	64	21.2
Some Post-Graduate Education	43	14.2
Master's Degree	142	47.0
Advanced Graduate or Professional Degree	15	5.0
Total	302	100

Table 17. Industry Classification

Industry	Frequency	Percent
Agriculture, Forestry, Fishing, and Hunting	2	0.6
Arts, Entertainment, and Recreation	3	1.0
Broadcasting and Communications	9	3.0
Colleges, Universities, and Professional Schools	16	5.3
Finance and Insurance	54	18.0
Healthcare and Social Assistance	46	15.3
Information (other services)	9	3.0
Management Consulting Services (including HRD consulting)	10	3.3
Manufacturing	34	11.3
Public Administration (including government)	9	3.0
Real Estate and Rental and Leasing	1	0.3
Retail Trade	14	4.7
Software Publishing	6	2.0
Transportation and Warehousing	11	3.6
Utilities	6	2.0
Wholesale Trade	5	1.7
Other	66	21.9
Total	301	100

Given that much of this survey solicited open-ended responses, the following summarizes the content themes of the responses to selected questions.

Question 1:

A: *Have you used the Model to enhance your career or to enhance the careers of professionals who work in your organization?*

More than half (55 percent) of the respondents indicated that they have used the 2004 Model to enhance their careers or the careers of individuals who work in their respective organizations.

B: *How have you used the Model to enhance your career?*

Of the 129 respondents who answered "yes" to Question A, 64 percent provided comments. Certification-related uses of the Model were the single highest category cited in response to this question. Other representative uses of the Model cited included:

- using the Model for self-assessment and professional development (27 percent of respondents)
- using the Model to identify gaps in learning for work teams (19 percent)
- planning career development options for new hires (14 percent)
- learning about benchmarks in self-assessment (9 percent)
- assessing the current skills of learning teams (7 percent).

Question 2:

What trends will have the biggest impact on training and development competencies in the future (in the next three to five years)?

Of the 102 comments citing future trends, the following themes arose most often:

- technology
- online learning
- increased use of social media
- social learning outside of the classroom
- informal learning
- mobile devices (tools and technology)
- more formal training of "learning enablers."

In addition to determining how the Model addresses the needs of the profession as a whole, another goal of this survey was to determine how well the Model and its associated products ultimately address the needs of employers who hire training and development professionals. The population most capable of addressing this question consists of high-level training and development professionals within organizations. These individuals are presumed to have a perspective on how well the Model addresses the needs of the training and development function of their organization as a whole (as opposed to how it addresses the needs of an individual professional).

Survey respondents capable of informing the "employer" perspective were defined as those in a senior-level manager role or those in an executive role in the organization (these respondents are referred to as "high-level respondents"). It is reasonable to expect that such respondents are either responsible for, or play a role in, hiring training and development professionals. Seventy-three respondents (24 percent of all respondents) to the product survey fit these criteria. Demographic information for these respondents is provided in Tables 18-20.

Table 18. Age of High-Level Respondents

Age	Frequency	Percent
29 or less	1	1.4
30 to 39	10	13.7
40 to 49	26	35.6
50 to 59	30	41.1
60 or over	6	8.2
Total	73	100

Table 19. Years of Experience in the Training and Development Profession

Years of Experience	Frequency	Percent
1 to 2 years	1	1.4
3 to 5 years	6	8.2
6 to 10 years	13	17.8
11 to 15 years	11	15.1
16 to 20 years	14	19.2
More than 20 years	28	38.4
Total	73	100

Table 20. Highest Level of Education Achieved

Educational Background	Frequency	Percent
Some University/College Education	2	2.8
University/College Graduate	13	18.1
Some Post-Graduate Education	7	9.7
Master's Degree	44	61.1
Advanced Graduate or Professional Degree	6	8.3
Total	72	100

Approximately 55 percent of the respondents in this sample have used the ASTD Competency Model to enhance their careers or the careers of those working for them. This appendix provides specific comments pertaining to how respondents in this subsample used the Model for their employees and their organization.

A number of respondents in this subsample commented on future trends. One executive noted that the Chief Learning Officer (CLO) role may more commonly be absorbed into the Human Resources (HR) Vice President (VP) role in coming years. This has the potential to adversely affect the field, as most HR executives do not have deep knowledge in this field. Others noted the transition from "trainer" to "learner enabler" or "facilitator." Multiple respondents mentioned the importance of using metrics that show the effect of their work so that a better case can be made for preserving the training and development function in the midst of organizational budget cuts. Many of these respondents, similar to the broader sample, indicated that online learning and related concepts would become even more important in the near future.

Finally, the survey asked respondents for any additional comments. One comment from a senior executive was very complimentary of the 2004 Competency Model:

> *The current 2004 ASTD Competency Model was well designed and much more effective than the prior model. In my role of VP, Talent Management I have often utilized the Model and the CPLP program in many applications for WLP team strategy, development, collaboration, and so on. On a broader level, I encourage ASTD to continue world-class focus on L&D, and to extend our expertise and image within the HR/Integrated Talent Management arena. We need to continue our growth beyond the "training" persona. The ASTD Competency Model is a priority tool to communicate and develop our members in these areas. Thanks for the GREAT work!*

Data from the competency survey was also used to evaluate whether high-level respondents viewed the importance of the AOEs differently than the broader population. Results of this analysis indicated that high-level respondents did not view the importance of the AOEs any differently than the broader population.

After the research team gained a solid perspective of the general views of the Model, they conducted a more in-depth audit of the Competency Model content relying on a focus group methodology.

Focus Groups

Through ASTD's database of certificants, the research team identified two groups of subject matter experts (SMEs). The first group, identified through ASTD's partnerships in the industry, consisted of 22 high-level, strategic thought leaders in the field. These individuals provided a high-level examination of the highest-level content to determine if there were gaps or errors. Following this review, the research team leveraged ASTD's database of CPLP credential holders to recruit 45 highly experienced training and development professionals to review and refine the proposed updates to the Competency Model. All of the SMEs had significant experience in the field, consistent with the review sessions conducted as part of the 2004 Competency Study (Bernthal et al., 2004).

The focus group sessions addressed a) whether the new content was comprehensively covered, b) whether any of the content should be divided or consolidated, c) suggestions for rewording any of the new content, and d) how to incorporate the new content into the existing content outline. The researchers conducted multiple two-hour review sessions per AOE with four to six SMEs in each session.

These detailed review sessions focused on the specific content underlying the Model. Again, the purpose of these conversations was to determine whether the content was relevant, accurate, or contained any gaps. Groups generally attempted to reach consensus; however, there were occasions in which they could not. In those circumstances, the researchers tabled the question, conducted additional background work, and then came back to the group with a recommendation. All disagreements were successfully resolved in this manner.

Validation Survey

Upon completion of the review of the Competency Model content by a large and diverse number of experts through preliminary surveys and focus groups, the research team developed a verification survey to send to the broader training and development profession as a whole. This survey was similar in design to the initial pulse check survey in that it asked for judgments about the relative importance of the competencies, AOEs, and key knowledge and actions. Furthermore, this survey incorporated an international perspective. Thus, while the research team encouraged subject matter experts to consider international implications throughout the Model revision process, the validation survey was an opportunity to determine if the Model truly was appropriate for international populations.

Generally, results were consistent with those the research team had observed in the pulse check surveys. Furthermore, a direct comparison between the ratings made by domestic and international respondents showed virtually no difference between the two groups. Results from the validation survey can be found in appendix C.

Foundational Competencies

ASTD's 2004 Study identified 12 competencies as essential for the majority of individuals across all professions. The competencies were termed "Foundational." The research team compared these Foundational Competencies against those that have been developed for similar professions. The researchers also compared them to broadly accepted Foundational Competencies such as those published by the U.S. Department of Labor and the Partnership for 21st Century Skills.

Generally, and as expected, ASTD's Foundational Competencies are consistent with those described in the above sources. Nonetheless, a review of the sources above yielded some recommended additions to the current Foundational Competencies set:

- Ethics (or, similarly, values/integrity) should be described broadly within the "Building Trust" competency.
- Innovation should be explicitly addressed.

Although the Foundational Competencies generally do a very good job of covering those skills required for successful performance across the field, the information-gathering activities associated with this study suggest that some of these competencies may require additional elaboration to emphasize their importance to the field. In particular, a number of stakeholders indicated the importance of demonstrating business acumen and understanding the needs of the organization when designing instructional strategies. An additional competency that may warrant further emphasis is cultural orientation.

All of the data collection feedback and recommendations were considered during the creation of the 2013 ASTD Competency Model.

Validation Survey Results

AOE Importance—High Level

For each of the Areas of Expertise (AOEs) listed, please indicate its importance to successful performance of YOUR JOB *now* and in the next *three* years (rank ordered by highest to lowest mean by current importance). Make your ratings on a scale from 1 (unnecessary) to 5 (essential). Mark 0 if not applicable.

AOE		Current Importance								
		0	1	2	3	4	5	*N*	*M*	*SD*
Instructional Design	#	11	21	60	142	322	851	1,407	4.34	1.01
	%	0.8	1.5	4.3	10.1	22.9	60.5	100		
Training Delivery	#	22	23	58	145	290	859	1,397	4.32	1.09
	%	1.6	1.6	4.2	10.4	20.8	61.5	100		
Performance Improvement	#	26	46	117	277	368	530	1,364	3.84	1.23
	%	1.9	3.4	8.6	20.3	27.0	38.9	100		
Evaluating Learning Impact	#	18	89	181	340	335	397	1,360	3.53	1.29
	%	1.3	6.5	13.3	25.0	24.6	29.2	100		
Change Management	#	51	75	191	266	342	422	1,347	3.51	1.4
	%	3.8	5.6	14.2	19.7	25.4	31.3	100		
Managing Learning Programs	#	71	61	162	295	310	412	1,311	3.49	1.43
	%	5.4	4.7	12.4	22.5	23.6	31.4	100		
Coaching	#	71	98	185	337	299	320	1,310	3.26	1.44
	%	5.4	7.5	14.1	25.7	22.8	24.4	100		
Integrated Talent Management	#	136	162	256	282	243	224	1,303	2.77[1]	1.57
	%	10.4	12.4	19.6	21.6	18.6	17.2	100		
Knowledge Management	#	54	123	243	356	281	245	1,302	3.09	1.38
	%	4.1	9.4	18.7	27.3	21.6	18.8	100		

[1] This AOE was rated important to very important in subsequent validation efforts and was therefore not eliminated.

AOE		Future Importance								
		0	1	2	3	4	5	*N*	*M*	*SD*
Instructional Design	#	8	21	52	107	275	922	1,385	4.44	0.96
	%	0.6	1.5	3.8	7.7	19.9	66.6	100		
Training Delivery	#	21	27	66	140	253	863	1,370	4.31	1.12
	%	1.5	2.0	4.8	10.2	18.5	63.0	100		
Performance Improvement	#	17	20	43	148	357	748	1,333	4.29	1.03
	%	1.3	1.5	3.2	11.1	26.8	56.1	100		
Evaluating Learning Impact	#	10	26	69	193	392	644	1,334	4.15	1.05
	%	0.7	1.9	5.2	14.5	29.4	48.3	100		
Change Management	#	32	46	95	202	352	606	1,333	3.96	1.26
	%	2.4	3.5	7.1	15.2	26.4	45.5	100		
Managing Learning Programs	#	49	37	81	199	355	562	1,283	3.92	1.31
	%	3.8	2.9	6.3	15.5	27.7	43.8	100		
Coaching	#	42	50	97	237	365	501	1,292	3.81	1.31
	%	3.3	3.9	7.5	18.3	28.3	38.8	100		
Integrated Talent Management	#	103	86	135	234	296	426	1,280	3.42	1.58
	%	8.0	6.7	10.5	18.3	23.1	33.3	100		
Knowledge Management	#	39	57	112	228	371	477	1,284	3.76	1.32
	%	3.0	4.4	8.7	17.8	28.9	37.1	100		

AOE Importance—Detailed Level

The tables that follow provide the *top three* key knowledge and key actions for each AOE, as ranked by current order of importance. Ratings were made on a scale from 1 (unnecessary) to 5 (essential) or 0 if not applicable.

List the importance of key knowledge and behaviors to successful performance of YOUR JOB *now* and in the next *three* years for:

Instructional Design

		Current Importance					Future Importance				
AOE	Key Knowledge or Action	*N*	Min	Max	*M*	*SD*	*N*	Min	Max	*M*	*SD*
Instructional Design—Key Knowledge	Various instructional methods (e.g., discussion, exercise, self-directed learning).	313	0	5	4.26	0.96	304	0	5	4.44	0.84
Instructional Design—Key Knowledge	Content knowledge or techniques to elicit content from subject matter experts.	313	1	5	4.16	0.96	303	0	5	4.27	0.90
Instructional Design—Key Knowledge	Instructional design theory and process.	313	1	5	4.00	1.01	302	0	5	4.10	1.03

		Current Importance					Future Importance				
AOE	Key Knowledge or Action	*N*	Min	Max	*M*	*SD*	*N*	Min	Max	*M*	*SD*
Instructional Design—Key Actions	Designs instructional material—Selects, modifies, or creates an appropriate design and development model or plan for a given project; identifies and documents measurable learning objectives; selects and uses a variety of techniques to define, structure, and sequence the instructional content and strategies; designs instructional content to reflect an understanding of the diversity of learners or groups of learners.	285	0	5	4.35	0.96	276	0	5	4.44	0.91
Instructional Design—Key Actions	Designs a curriculum, program, or learning solution—Uses a variety of techniques for determining instructional content; creates or partners with others to plan and design the curriculum, program, or learning solution; designs an experience that enables informal learning.	283	0	5	4.28	1.04	276	0	5	4.46	0.86
Instructional Design—Key Actions	Develops instructional materials—Selects or modifies existing instructional materials or develops new instructional materials; conducts review of materials with appropriate parties, such as subject matter experts, design team, and the target audience; creates logical learning units/objects as appropriate; designs or builds assets (e.g., role plays, self-assessment tests) to support the learning experience and meet objectives as appropriate; develops instructional content to reflect an understanding of the diversity of learners or groups of learners.	284	0	5	4.28	0.99	277	0	5	4.34	0.96

Training Delivery

		Current Importance					Future Importance				
AOE	Key Knowledge or Action	*N*	Min	Max	*M*	*SD*	*N*	Min	Max	*M*	*SD*
Training Delivery—Key Knowledge	Facilitation and presentation techniques and tools.	417	0	5	4.35	0.93	407	0	5	4.38	0.91
Training Delivery—Key Knowledge	Various instructional methods (e.g., discussion, exercises, self-directed learning).	410	0	5	4.31	0.91	404	1	5	4.47	0.78
Training Delivery—Key Knowledge	Familiarity with content being taught and how the solution addresses the need (i.e., context).	416	0	5	4.24	0.95	410	0	5	4.34	0.90

		Current Importance					Future Importance				
AOE	Key Knowledge or Action	*N*	Min	Max	*M*	*SD*	*N*	Min	Max	*M*	*SD*
Training Delivery—Key Actions	Creates a positive learning climate—Establishes a learning environment where learners feel safe to try new skills and behaviors, where individual differences are respected, and confidentiality is supported; personally models behavior that is consistent with the goals of the program.	373	0	5	4.50	0.90	364	0	5	4.56	0.85
Training Delivery—Key Actions	Facilitates learning—Varies delivery style to fit the audience; adapts to the needs of learners and adjusts curriculum as needed; presents information in a logical sequence; uses appropriate visual aids; listens and responds to questions and objections; leverages the knowledge and experience of participants to facilitate learning; manages group dynamics; manages time on learning topics.	374	0	5	4.49	0.93	369	0	5	4.58	0.83
Training Delivery—Key Actions	Encourages participation and builds learner motivation—Uses techniques and skills to engage all participants in the learning experience; adapts own style to different learner and group styles; makes effort to "bring in" passive participants; creates excitement and commitment to the learning experience; engages learners by providing opportunities for participation and experimentation in the learning process; capitalizes on participant diversity to maximize learning; builds a collaborative learning environment.	375	0	5	4.43	0.92	368	0	5	4.54	0.85

Performance Improvement

		Current Importance					Future Importance				
AOE	Key Knowledge or Action	*N*	Min	Max	*M*	*SD*	*N*	Min	Max	*M*	*SD*
Performance Improvement—Key Knowledge	Performance improvement process.	97	0	5	4.07	1.06	95	1	5	4.44	0.87
Performance Improvement—Key Knowledge	Performance analysis (e.g., business analysis, performance gap assessment, and cause analysis).	94	0	5	4.04	1.16	91	0	5	4.44	0.96
Performance Improvement—Key Knowledge	Communication techniques (e.g., adapting message to the audience, using a variety of channels).	91	0	5	3.97	1.14	92	1	5	4.28	0.98

AOE	Key Knowledge or Action	Current Importance					Future Importance				
		N	Min	Max	*M*	*SD*	*N*	Min	Max	*M*	*SD*
Performance Improvement—Key Actions	Builds and sustains relationships—Builds credibility and trust with the client based on knowledge and understanding of the business; partners and collaborates with the client on an ongoing basis to maintain a sustained business relationship.	85	2	5	4.31	0.87	85	2	5	4.53	0.83
Performance Improvement—Key Actions	Selects solutions—Recommends appropriate human performance improvement solutions that address the root cause(s) of performance gaps rather than symptoms or side effects; presents recommended changes to the client and helps them assess cost, time, and risk considerations.	85	0	5	4.04	1.16	84	0	5	4.26	1.00
Performance Improvement—Key Actions	Incorporates customer/stakeholder needs—Partners with the customer/stakeholder to clarify needs, business goals, and objectives; agrees on desired results and gains agreement on how those results can be achieved efficiently and effectively.	83	1	5	4.02	1.04	82	1	5	4.32	0.89

Evaluating Learning Impact

AOE	Key Knowledge or Action	Current Importance					Future Importance				
		N	Min	Max	*M*	*SD*	*N*	Min	Max	*M*	*SD*
Measurement and Metrics—Key Knowledge	Interpretation and reporting of data.	26	0	5	4.15	1.22	26	3	5	4.77	0.51
Measurement and Metrics—Key Knowledge	Learning analytics and relevant metrics.	28	0	5	3.89	1.29	27	3	5	4.52	0.64
Measurement and Metrics—Key Knowledge	Theories and types of evaluations at the training, program, organizational/system level.	28	0	5	3.46	1.40	27	2	5	4.07	1.00
Measurement and Metrics—Key Actions	Analyzes and interprets data—Creates summaries of data in a format that can be readily understood and communicated in order to facilitate decision making; adheres to rules of statistical analysis to reduce bias and provide adequate support for conclusions; uses a process of creative inquiry to fully explore the data and all of its possible implications and meaning.	26	1	5	4.19	1.02	26	3	5	4.50	0.71

		Current Importance					Future Importance				
AOE	Key Knowledge or Action	*N*	Min	Max	*M*	*SD*	*N*	Min	Max	*M*	*SD*
Measurement and Metrics—Key Actions	Identifies customer expectations—Works with customers or stakeholders to determine why they are interested in measurement and what they hope to accomplish with the results; clearly defines research questions, expectations, resources available, and desired outcomes of the measurement project; manages unrealistic expectations.	26	2	5	4.00	1.02	26	2	5	4.27	0.92
Measurement and Metrics—Key Actions	Selects appropriate strategies, research design, and measures—Uses customer questions and expectations to guide the selection of appropriate strategies, research designs, and quantitative and qualitative measurement tools; employs a variety of measures and methods to reduce bias and ensure objective conclusions; identifies appropriate sample sizes, data tracking methods, and reporting formats; balances practical implications of rigor, effort, real-life constraints, and objectivity to create a workable approach; identifies information that indicates whether the program is on track.	26	2	5	3.92	0.98	26	3	5	4.19	0.80

Change Management

		Current Importance					Future Importance				
AOE	Key Knowledge or Action	*N*	Min	Max	*M*	*SD*	*N*	Min	Max	*M*	*SD*
Facilitating Organizational Change—Key Knowledge	Organizational systems and culture, including political dynamics in organizational settings.	72	0	5	4.35	0.98	71	2	5	4.59	0.67
Facilitating Organizational Change—Key Knowledge	Change theory and change models.	72	0	5	4.15	1.02	72	2	5	4.39	0.80
Facilitating Organizational Change—Key Knowledge	Systems thinking and open systems theory (i.e., organization is an open system influenced by the external environment).	72	0	5	4.08	1.06	71	2	5	4.42	0.84
Facilitating Organizational Change—Key Actions	Establishes sponsorship and ownership for change—Clarifies case for change and desired outcomes; facilitates client sponsorship of expected outcomes; engages stakeholders to build critical mass of support.	63	0	5	4.49	0.86	63	3	5	4.73	0.52

		Current Importance					Future Importance				
AOE	Key Knowledge or Action	*N*	Min	Max	*M*	*SD*	*N*	Min	Max	*M*	*SD*
Facilitating Organizational Change—Key Actions	Builds involvement—Involves people to raise awareness and gathers input on the best course of action; helps clients and change leaders build involvement and ownership in the change process; helps clients create a communication plan that generates buy-in and commitment; facilitates effective two-way communications to ensure understanding, commitment, and behavior change.	61	0	5	4.44	0.94	62	3	5	4.69	0.56
Facilitating Organizational Change—Key Actions	Facilitates strategic planning for change—Facilitates creation of overall change strategy with sponsor and key change leaders; clarifies what must change, how to minimize the human impact and optimize buy-in; helps identify all technical, organizational, cultural, and people-related change initiatives; shapes the best process and conditions to accomplish results; designs appropriate change process plans to be time efficient and responsive to needs.	62	0	5	4.40	0.93	62	3	5	4.65	0.60

Managing Learning Programs

		Current Importance					Future Importance				
AOE	Key Knowledge or Action	*N*	Min	Max	*M*	*SD*	*N*	Min	Max	*M*	*SD*
Managing the Learning Function—Key Knowledge	Principles of management and leadership.	197	0	5	4.25	0.99	192	0	5	4.49	0.81
Managing the Learning Function—Key Knowledge	Training and development-related programs being administered in the organization.	200	0	5	4.21	0.91	192	1	5	4.37	0.78
Managing the Learning Function—Key Knowledge	Organization's business model, drivers, and competitive position in the industry.	205	0	5	3.86	1.22	198	1	5	4.27	0.96
Managing the Learning Function—Key Actions	Implements action plans—Converts the training and development strategies into action plans; balances or reconciles strategy with real-life constraints of the workplace; creates a reasonable timeline that conforms to the expectations of customers/stakeholders.	193	0	5	4.33	0.96	187	3	5	4.65	0.57

		Current Importance					Future Importance				
AOE	Key Knowledge or Action	*N*	Min	Max	*M*	*SD*	*N*	Min	Max	*M*	*SD*
Managing the Learning Function—Key Actions	Establishes a vision—Creates a picture of how the learning function can improve the performance of the business and enable execution of the organization's strategy; partners with business unit leaders to advocate for improving human performance through the learning function.	193	0	5	4.30	0.94	182	3	5	4.66	0.58
Managing the Learning Function—Key Actions	Establishes strategies—Develops long-range learning, development, and human performance strategies to implement the vision; understands what drives the business and determines how the learning function can best add value.	191	0	5	4.29	0.98	185	2	5	4.65	0.57

Coaching

		Current Importance					Future Importance				
AOE	Key Knowledge or Action	*N*	Min	Max	*M*	*SD*	*N*	Min	Max	*M*	*SD*
Coaching—Key Knowledge	Communicating effectively.	60	3	5	4.77	0.53	58	3	5	4.84	0.45
Coaching—Key Knowledge	Co-creating the relationship and building trust.	60	3	5	4.67	0.60	57	3	5	4.74	0.55
Coaching—Key Knowledge	Facilitating learning and results.	59	3	5	4.46	0.65	58	2	5	4.64	0.61
Coaching—Key Actions	Demonstrates active listening—Focuses completely on what the client is saying and is not saying to understand the meaning of what is said in the context of the client's desires and to support client self-expression.	57	2	5	4.68	0.69	54	2	5	4.76	0.61
Coaching—Key Actions	Asks powerful questions—Asks questions that reveal the information needed for maximum benefit to the coaching relationship and the client.	58	2	5	4.55	0.73	56	2	5	4.63	0.68
Coaching—Key Actions	Uses direct communication—Communicates effectively during coaching sessions and uses language that has the greatest positive impact on the client.	58	2	5	4.53	0.86	55	2	5	4.69	0.66

Integrated Talent Management

AOE	Key Knowledge or Action	Current Importance					Future Importance				
		N	Min	Max	*M*	*SD*	*N*	Min	Max	*M*	*SD*
Integrated Talent Management—Key Knowledge	Key components of talent management systems (i.e., workforce planning and talent acquisition, performance management, employee development, succession planning, compensation and rewards, engagement and retention).	33	0	5	4.42	1.03	31	3	5	4.77	0.50
Integrated Talent Management—Key Knowledge	Individual and organizational assessment tools.	35	0	5	4.03	1.18	33	2	5	4.36	0.86
Integrated Talent Management—Key Actions	Equips managers to develop their people—Educates managers about performance management skills; provides development tools for managers; helps managers promote employee engagement; holds managers accountable for developing talent; enables employees to take responsibility for their own development.	32	0	5	4.28	1.11	30	3	5	4.63	0.56
Integrated Talent Management—Key Actions	Organizes delivery of developmental resources—Provides flexible access to multiple vehicles for developing talent (e.g., training, online learning, social media, coaching, job rotation, stretch and expatriate assignments); selects and manages training suppliers and consultants; monitors delivery of solutions to ensure successful implementation; plans and manages resources to ensure adequate coverage.	32	0	5	3.81	1.20	28	3	5	4.18	0.67
Integrated Talent Management—Key Actions	Supports engagement and retention efforts—Integrates training and development opportunities into the organization's retention strategy; measures employee engagement; involves experienced employees in coaching and mentoring programs; recognizes and leverages generational differences.	32	0	5	3.81	1.28	30	2	5	4.33	0.80
Integrated Talent Management—Key Actions	Aligns talent management to organizational objectives—Works with leaders and business unit heads to ensure that talent management supports key organizational objectives; aligns and integrates training and development with key talent management processes.	32	0	5	4.31	1.15	30	4	5	4.73	0.45

Knowledge Management

		Current Importance					Future Importance				
AOE	Key Knowledge or Action	*N*	Min	Max	*M*	*SD*	*N*	Min	Max	*M*	*SD*
Knowledge Management—Key Knowledge	Knowledge management best practices.	17	0	5	4.00	1.32	16	3	5	4.25	0.86
Knowledge Management—Key Knowledge	Knowledge management concepts, philosophy, and theory.	18	0	5	3.72	1.74	17	2	5	4.12	0.99
Knowledge Management—Key Knowledge	Existing and emerging technologies that enable knowledge sharing (e.g., online collaborative workspaces, mobile technologies).	17	0	5	3.53	1.51	16	2	5	4.25	1.07
Knowledge Management—Key Actions	Advocates knowledge management (KM)—Develops the KM vision and strategy, ensuring that it integrates with the organization's business strategy; helps the organization understand the concept and value of effective knowledge creation, sharing and reuse; assists senior management in building and communicating personal commitment and advocacy for KM; helps promote the knowledge agenda.	17	0	5	3.59	1.50	16	1	5	4.19	1.28
Knowledge Management—Key Actions	Leverages technology—Assesses, selects, and applies current and emerging information, learning tools, and technologies to support work-related learning and the development of knowledge.	17	0	5	3.53	1.70	16	3	5	4.50	0.82
Knowledge Management—Key Actions	Transforms knowledge into learning—Assesses organizational learning capabilities; uses knowledge capture and sharing as ways to enhance organization-wide learning; facilitates drawing tacit knowledge from experts (knowledge that experts have but cannot articulate) and makes it explicit knowledge so that others can learn it.	17	0	5	3.53	1.94	16	2	5	4.31	1.01

Validation Survey Demographics

Primary Area of Expertise

From the following list, please select the one Area of Expertise (i.e., professional/ technical competency) in which you have the most expertise.

AOE	Frequency	Percent
Performance Improvement	93	7.1
Instructional Design	337	25.7
Training Delivery	434	33.1
Evaluating Learning Impact	27	2.1
Managing Learning Programs	209	15.9
Integrated Talent Management	34	2.6
Coaching	60	4.6
Knowledge Management	19	1.4
Change Management	72	5.5
I do not have expertise in any of these areas.	28	2.1
Total	1,313	100

Age

Age	Frequency	Percent
29 or less	31	2.7
30 to 39	209	18.3
40 to 49	349	30.6
50 to 59	379	33.2
60 or over	154	13.5
Would rather not say	19	1.7
Total	1,141	100

Gender

Gender	Frequency	Percent
Female	744	65.1
Male	384	33.6
Would rather not say	15	1.3
Total	1,143	100

Years of Experience in the T&D Profession

Years of Experience	Frequency	Percent
Less than 1 year	12	1.0
1 to 2 years	40	3.5
3 to 5 years	113	9.9
6 to 10 years	196	17.1
11 to 15 years	228	19.9
16 to 20 years	197	17.2
21 to 30 years	259	22.7
More than 30 years	98	8.6
Total	1,143	100

Career Role and Skill Level

Career Role and Skill Level	Frequency	Percent
Entry-Level	22	1.9
Mid-Level Specialist	141	12.4
Senior-Level Specialist	317	27.8
Entry-Level Manager	46	4.0
Mid-Level Manager	239	20.9
Senior-Level Manager	159	13.9
Entry- to Mid-Level Executive	64	5.6
Mid- to Senior-Level Executive	153	13.4
Total	1,141	100

Educational Background

Please indicate the HIGHEST LEVEL of education you have achieved.

Education	Frequency	Percent
High school diploma/certificate or equivalent (i.e., prior to university)	5	0.4
Some trade/business school training (may include special degrees or certifications)	21	1.8
Two-year degree (e.g., trade or business school certificate/degree/ associate of arts degree)	23	2.0
Some university/college education	64	5.6
University/college graduate (e.g., bachelor of arts, bachelor of sciences)	217	19.0
Some post-graduate education	137	12.0
Master's degree (e.g., master of arts, master of sciences, master of business administration)	564	49.3
Advanced graduate or professional degree (e.g., doctor of philosophy, doctor of medicine)	112	9.8
None of the above	1	0.1
Total	1,144	100

Primary Area of Job Responsibility

Please identify which ONE of the following BEST describes your major area of responsibility.

Job Responsibility	Frequency	Percent
Training Delivery	249	21.8
Instructional Design	252	22.1
Career Development	30	2.6
Coaching	13	1.1
Leadership Development, Management Development, Executive Development	171	15.0
Performance Consulting	73	6.4
Change Management, Organization Development, Organizational Effectiveness	113	9.9
Knowledge Management	27	2.4
Measurement and Evaluation	19	1.7
Human Capital/Talent Management	44	3.9
Educational Technology	31	2.7
Human Resource Management	27	2.4
Other specific Human Resource responsibility	91	8.0
Total	1,140	100

Organization Type

Which of the following best describes your organization?

Organization Type	Frequency	Percent
For profit organization	602	52.9
Nonprofit (not including government, academic, or military)	185	16.3
Academic institution	53	4.7
Government agency	79	6.9
Military branch or service	11	1.0
Consulting firm	79	6.9
Independent consultant or sole proprietor	48	4.2
Other, please specify	80	7.0
Total	1,137	100

Industry

Please select ONE industry classification that BEST describes where you conduct most of your work.

Industry	Frequency	Percent
Agriculture, Forestry, Fishing, and Hunting	8	0.7
Arts, Entertainment, and Recreation (including Lodging/ Hospitality)	22	1.9
Broadcasting and Communications	6	0.5
Business Schools and Computer Management Training	1	0.1
Colleges, Universities, and Professional Schools	32	2.8
Education	71	6.3
Finance and Insurance	175	15.4
Healthcare and Social Assistance	165	14.6
Information (other services)	32	2.8
Management Consulting Services (including HRD consulting)	67	5.9
Manufacturing	136	12.0
National Security	15	1.3
Public Administration (including government)	43	3.8
Real Estate and Rental and Leasing	12	1.1
Retail Trade	31	2.7
Software Publishing	16	1.4
Transportation and Warehousing	21	1.9
Utilities	41	3.6
Wholesale Trade	4	0.4
Other (please specify)	236	20.8
Total	1,134	100

Country

Country	Frequency	Percent
New Zealand	3	0.2
Egypt	4	0.2
Italy	2	0.1
Brazil	3	0.2
Netherlands	10	0.6
Hong Kong	6	0.3
Malaysia	6	0.3
Indonesia	3	0.2
Jamaica	2	0.1
Philippines	3	0.2
Kuwait	2	0.1
Switzerland	6	0.3
United States	1,550	87.0
Saudi Arabia	6	0.3
Australia	13	0.7
United Kingdom	8	0.4
Mexico	2	0.1
Korea, Republic of	2	0.1
Trinidad and Tobago	2	0.1
China	10	0.6
Peru	3	0.2
India	19	1.1
United Arab Emirates	5	0.3
Israel	2	0.1
Canada	48	2.7
Thailand	2	0.1
France	3	0.2
Belgium	2	0.1
Japan	9	0.5
Spain	3	0.2
Turkey	2	0.1
Denmark	5	0.3
Romania	3	0.2
Pakistan	2	0.1
Singapore	7	0.4
South Africa	6	0.3
Other responses	18	1.0
Total	1,782	100

APPENDIX D

Foundational Competencies Dictionary

Table of Contents

Foundational Competencies

1. Business Skills

Analyzing Needs and Proposing Solutions

Indentifies and understands business issues and client needs, problems, and opportunities; compares data from different sources to draw conclusions; uses effective approaches for choosing a course of action or developing appropriate solutions; takes action that is consistent with available facts, constraints, and probable consequences.

Key Actions

Gathers information about client needs—Collects information to better understand client needs, issues, problems, and opportunities; reviews organizational information and performance outcomes; studies organizational systems to better understand the factors affecting performance; integrates information from a variety of sources; asks internal and external partners for input and insight.

Diagnoses learning and development issues—Uses research methods to isolate the causes of learning and development problems; proposes theories to understand and explain the factors affecting performance; detects trends, associations, and cause-effect relationships.

Generates multiple alternatives—Gathers information about best practices; thinks expansively and brainstorms multiple approaches; generates relevant options for addressing problems/opportunities and achieving desired outcomes; maintains a database or bank of possible solutions and their effectiveness.

Searches for innovative solutions—Challenges paradigms and looks for innovative alternatives; draws upon diverse sources for ideas and inspiration in creative problem-solving activities.

Chooses appropriate solution(s)—Formulates clear decision criteria; evaluates options by considering implications, risks, feasibility, and consequences on the client system and on other parts of the organization; prioritizes and chooses an effective option.

Recognizes impact—Considers the implications of learning and development decisions, solutions, and strategies in other contexts; makes decisions using a broad range of knowledge that extends beyond the limitations of the organization and its immediate needs.

Proposes solution(s)—Recommends a plan or process for making changes; clearly explains rationale for the recommended solution and how it will address the performance gap or opportunity.

Applying Business Skills

Understands the organization's business strategies, key metrics, and financial goals; uses economic, financial, and organizational data to build and document the business case for investing in learning solutions; uses business terminology when communicating with others.

Key Actions

Understands the business—Understands the organization's business model and competitive position in the marketplace; understands how the business is leveraging core competencies for growth and profitability; understands the value proposition to external customers.

Understands business operations—Understands the organization's structure, systems, functions, and processes; understands how the organization operates, including its planning processes, decision-making channels, and information management systems; understands how products and services are developed, sold, and delivered to customers.

Applies financial data—Understands financial statements and how to interpret them; accurately tracks and forecasts revenues and expenses.

Uses business terminology to gain credibility—Translates learning and development verbiage into business terminology that stakeholders will understand and relate to; speaks the language of the business when applying professional expertise.

Recognizes business priorities—Tracks the changing needs and expectations of external customers; identifies links between internal demands and external needs; works to understand the business priorities of internal clients and how the learning function could help them achieve greater success.

Creates a value proposition—Establishes the link between business needs and specific solutions; documents how solutions will achieve targeted business results; identifies outcomes that will result from implementing learning and development solutions; creates a compelling business case.

Advances the learning and development business agenda—Understands how decisions are made in the organizational structure and how power is exercised; recognizes key stakeholders and their priorities; leverages understanding of politics across business units and decision makers; presents and defends the business value of learning and development solutions.

Driving Results

Identifies opportunities for improvement and sets well-defined goals related to learning and development solutions; orchestrates efforts and measures progress; strives to achieve/exceed goals and produces exceptional results.

Key Actions

Targets improvement opportunities—Systematically evaluates business opportunities and targets those with the greatest potential for affecting results; identifies opportunities to improve organizational performance; continually seeks new ways of leveraging human performance to improve business results.

Establishes goals and objectives—Sets stretch goals to encourage higher performance; establishes objectives (e.g., SMART) to achieve reliable business results.

Orchestrates effort to achieve results—Mobilizes additional resources as needed and works tenaciously to achieve stretch goals.

Overcomes obstacles—Identifies obstacles to achieving the organization's strategy; anticipates and overcomes barriers; prevents irrelevant issues or distractions from interfering with the timely completion of important tasks.

Provides courageous leadership—Takes a stand and follows through with actions that support business objectives, even when those actions may be unpopular.

Planning and Implementing Assignments

Develops action plans, obtains resources, and completes assignments in a timely manner to ensure that learning and development goals are achieved.

Key Actions

Establishes parameters and forecasts outcomes—Identifies critical project parameters along with potential needs and trends that may affect success; agrees to action and commits resources based on careful consideration of possible future events.

Uses planning tools to create project plans—Uses planning tools such as Gantt charts, mind maps, risk analysis tools, and roles/responsibility matrices to create a practical action plan; identifies critical activities and assignments along with less-critical tasks; adjusts the project plan and priorities as needed.

Manages budget—Calculates projected costs and develops budget; monitors expenses relative to budgeted costs; adjusts spending and resource allocation as new challenges arise.

Determines tasks and resources—Determines project requirements by breaking them down into tasks and identifying types of equipment, materials, and persons needed.

Plans for contingencies—Proactively identifies potential problems and creates contingency plans or work-arounds to implement if problems occur.

Mobilizes resources—Takes advantage of available resources (people, processes, departments, and tools) to complete work efficiently; coordinates with internal and external partners.

Manages time—Allocates appropriate amounts of time for completing own and others' work; avoids scheduling conflicts; develops timelines and milestones and stays focused on achieving them.

Tracks progress and ensures completion—Monitors progress to ensure projects are completed on time and efficiently; follows up with individuals as needed to check progress; regularly communicates with stakeholders to ensure that promised goals have been achieved; identifies what is working well along with problems and obstacles; makes course corrections during the project.

Thinking Strategically

Understands internal and external factors that impact learning and development in organizations; keeps abreast of trends and anticipates opportunities to add value to the business; operates from a systems perspective in creating learning and development strategies; creates learning and development strategies that are in alignment with business goals.

Key Actions

Builds learning and development strategies in alignment with business goals—Develops both short- and long-term learning and development strategies that support the organization's strategic direction and are aligned with business goals; generates options to achieve these goals.

Builds strategic alignment—Contributes to the development and refinement of the organization's vision, goals, and strategies with a focus on maximizing talent; integrates and synthesizes other viewpoints to build alignment.

Understands external factors impacting learning and development—Understands the political, economic, sociological, cultural, and global factors that can affect an organization's performance in the marketplace; understands the context within which learning and development takes place in terms of government actions, legal requirements, and wider societal needs.

Understands the organizational context for learning and development—Understands how learning and development contribute to organizational success; understands the ways in which "people development" is implemented by line managers and functional specialists; understands how different aspects of HR and HRD are integrated with each other, the business strategy, and organizational structures.

Recognizes and acts on emerging opportunities—Anticipates how trends may impact and shape the learning and development industry; scans and monitors new developments in other fields and industries; shows curiosity about the business and challenges assumptions; seeks inspiration from different perspectives in constructing future scenarios; frames options for the learning and development function to add value to the business.

Operates from a systems perspective—Views the organization as a dynamic system; recognizes the need to understand and integrate interconnected elements; sees the big picture and complex relationships; recognizes patterns and broad implications of issues; balances long-term strategic goals with short-term priorities when making decisions.

Applying Innovation

Uses new resources, methods, tools, or content to advance learning and development; incorporates or applies new thinking or new techniques into learning and development solutions; applies existing techniques in new ways to enhance solutions, including those designed to more fully engage and support the learner.

Key Actions

Determines the latest advances—Scans the external environment for the latest developments inside and outside the learning and development industry (e.g., technology, social learning tools, mobile, gamification, simulations, new channels); determines if and in what context they should be applied.

Leverages new and existing tools and techniques—Leverages existing resources in new ways to enhance learning solutions; identifies opportunities to implement new learning methodologies or approaches appropriately; facilitates implementation; evaluates outcomes and impact.

Fosters an active evaluation process—Evaluates and revises new ideas and techniques prior to full implementation; evaluates new techniques and tools in terms of business objectives; monitors implementation.

2. Global Mindset

Appreciates and leverages the capabilities, insights, and ideas of all individuals; works effectively with individuals from different generations who have diverse styles, abilities, motivations, and/or backgrounds; works effectively across borders and cultures given the increasingly global workforce.

Key Actions

Accommodates cultural differences—Demonstrates awareness of differences in business customs and practices throughout the world; recognizes that people face additional comprehension and communication challenges when working in a second language; adjusts processes and expectations to facilitate their full participation in meetings, conference calls, workshops, etc.

Conveys respect for different perspectives—Shows respect both verbally and nonverbally by demonstrating consideration and appreciation of cultural concerns and expectations.

Expands own awareness—Establishes relationships with people from a variety of backgrounds; learns about differences in social norms, decision-making approaches, and preferences; encourages dialogue that promotes acceptance of different opinions; continually examines own biases and behaviors to avoid stereotypical responses.

Adapts behavior to accommodate others—Modifies behavior to help make others feel comfortable and accepted; accommodates different learning styles and preferences by providing a mixture of learning and development solutions.

Champions diversity—Advocates the value of diversity; takes actions to increase diversity in the workplace (for example, by recruiting and developing people from varied backgrounds and cultures); confronts inappropriate behavior by others; challenges exclusionary organizational practices.

Leverages diverse contributions—Solicits contributions from a diverse group of individuals; uses different perspectives to generate more creative problem solving; maximizes effectiveness by assigning work that capitalizes on people's unique talents and abilities.

3. Industry Knowledge

Actively scans and assesses information on current and emerging trends in the learning and development industry; develops and maintains knowledge of other industries, as appropriate.

Key Actions

Maintains own professional knowledge—Seeks relevant knowledge in areas beyond own current area(s) of expertise.

Keeps abreast of industry changes and trends—Monitors new developments in the learning and development industry; stays abreast of current and emerging trends; maintains memberships in relevant professional associations; joins learning communities to exchange industry information and ideas with others; attends professional meetings and conferences; reads professional publications.

Builds industry sector knowledge—Builds position-relevant knowledge of other industries or industry sectors, such as sales, service, finance, or pharmaceuticals; incorporates industry-specific knowledge into learning and development solutions; establishes credibility in other industries, as appropriate.

4. Interpersonal Skills

Building Trust

Interacts with others in a way that gives them confidence in one's intentions and those of the organization.

Key Actions

Operates with integrity—Demonstrates honesty and behaves according to ethical principles; ensures that words and actions are consistent; walks the talk; behaves dependably across situations.

Discloses position—Shares thoughts, feelings, and rationale so that others understand positions and policies.

Maintains confidentiality—Keeps private or sensitive information about others confidential.

Leads by example—Serves as a role model for the organization's values; takes responsibility for delivering on commitments; gives proper credit to others; acknowledges own mistakes rather than blaming others.

Treats people fairly—Treats all stakeholders with dignity, respect, and fairness; listens to others without prejudging; objectively considers others' ideas and opinions, even when they conflict with prescribed policies, procedures, or commonly held beliefs; champions the perspectives of different partners even in the face of resistance; engages in effective conflict resolution.

Ensures compliance with legal, ethical, and regulatory requirements—Ensures that processes and results comply with relevant legal, ethical, and regulatory requirements; monitors compliance and creates reports if needed.

Communicating Effectively

Expresses thoughts, feelings, and ideas in a clear, concise and compelling manner in both individual and group situations; actively listens to others; adjusts style to capture the attention of the audience; develops and deploys targeted communication strategies that inform and build support.

Key Actions

Develops and deploys effective communication strategies—Creates plans for communicating and leveraging information; employs diverse media to summarize and convey results.

Delivers clear messages—Uses appropriate vocabulary; understands the material and demonstrates command of the topic; logically and simply conveys ideas.

Presents with impact—Speaks with appropriate pace and inflection; conveys an air of confidence, ease, and enthusiasm; uses congruent nonverbal communication; uses visual aids to enhance understanding of the content.

Adjusts message content and delivery—Monitors audience reactions and adopts alternative strategies to improve overall impact; presents own message in different ways to enhance understanding; responds appropriately to questions and feedback.

Demonstrates active listening—Listens to others, interprets their message correctly; checks understanding; acknowledges different viewpoints.

Invites dialogue—Engages others in dialogue by using appropriate questioning techniques and involving others in conversations about things that matter; encourages people to express their hopes and fears; welcomes feedback.

Creates clear written communication—Writes clearly and understandably; sequences information in a logical manner to aid understanding; avoids jargon or technical words; uses a tone and format suggested by the topic and audience.

Masters multiple communication methods—Selects communication media and methods based on the needs of the recipients; adapts to virtual work situations involving remote workers who may use a range of communication styles and methods.

Influencing Stakeholders

Sells the value of learning or the recommended solution as a way of improving organizational performance; gains commitment to solutions that will improve individual, team, and organizational performance.

Key Actions

Analyzes stakeholder perspectives—Identifies key stakeholders, analyzes likely reactions, and determines how to address their unique needs and preferences.

Establishes a marketing strategy—Develops a strategy for presenting the business case and proposed solution; plans how to leverage supportive factors and overcome or minimize barriers; prepares a communication campaign.

Communicates a strong value proposition—Helps listeners understand how the proposed learning and development solution will achieve targeted business results; provides convincing rational based on the business case.

Builds energy and support—Encourages collaboration from people representing different levels and functions; invites people to participate in the decision-making process to obtain good input, create buy-in, and ensure understanding of the resulting decisions.

Gains commitment to the solution—Uses various influencing techniques to win support for the proposed learning solution; makes persuasive arguments, handles objections, negotiates key points, and summarizes outcomes; gains agreement to implement a solution or take partnership-oriented action.

Networking and Partnering

Develops and uses a network of collaborative relationships with internal and external contacts to leverage the learning and development strategy in a way that facilitates the accomplishment of business results.

Key Actions

Networks with others—Proactively builds a personal network of individuals and groups inside and outside of the organization who can provide quick advice or solutions; includes influential people (such as senior leaders, department heads, external vendors/suppliers) and learning and development experts.

Benchmarks and shares best practices—Maintains contacts with others outside of the organization to learn from their experiences and share best practices in learning and development.

Establishes common goals—Places priority on organizational goals and finding ways for partners to work together for the common goal; establishes common ground with learning and development goals to facilitate cooperation.

Develops partnering relationships—Establishes strong interpersonal relationships by staying in close contact with key individuals and working cooperatively; helps others feel valued and appreciated by monitoring their needs and exchanging occasional favors (for example, providing a sounding board to test proposals or learn what's happening in other parts of the industry).

Generates new collaborative possibilities—Seeks and expands on original ideas, enhances others' ideas, and contributes own ideas about the issues at hand; gains clarity about own thinking; expands options for future collaboration.

Emotional Intelligence

Perceives the emotional state of one's own self and others accurately and uses that information to help guide effective decision making and build positive working relationships.

Key Actions

Empathy—Listens intently; understands situation from another's point-of-view.

Nurtures Relationships—Demonstrates sincerity for people's contributions; sets a positive tone of cooperation; holds the interests of others in mind while focusing on win-win outcomes.

Self-Awareness—Focuses attention on one's own emotional state and assesses it accurately; uses self-awareness to guide decision making.

Self-Regulation—Chooses emotions that are constructive versus reactive; manages one's own emotional state.

5. Personal Skills

Demonstrating Adaptability

Maintains effectiveness when experiencing major changes in work tasks, the work environment, or conditions affecting the organization (for example, economic, political, cultural, or technological); remains open to new people, thoughts, and approaches; adjusts effectively to work within new work structures, processes, requirements, or cultures.

Key Actions

Seeks to understand changes—Seeks to understand changes in work tasks, situations, and environments as well as the logic or basis for change; actively seeks information about new work situations and withholds judgment.

Approaches change positively—Treats changes as opportunities for learning or growth; focuses on the beneficial aspects of change; speaks positively and advocates the change when it helps promote organizational goals and strategy.

Remains open to different ideas and approaches—Thinks expansively by remaining open to different lines of thought and approaches; readily tries new and different approaches in changing situations.

Adjusts behavior—Quickly modifies behavior to deal effectively with changes in the work environment; acquires new knowledge or skills to deal with the change; does not persist with ineffective behaviors; shows resiliency and maintains effectiveness even in the face of uncertainty or ambiguity.

Adapts to handle implementation challenges—Effectively handles global, cultural, economic, social, and political challenges to the effective implementation of learning and development solutions; works to overcome barriers and deal constructively with nontraditional or challenging situations.

Modeling Personal Development

Actively identifies new areas for one's own personal learning; regularly creates and takes advantage of learning opportunities; applies newly gained knowledge and skill on the job.

Key Actions

Models self-mastery in learning—Serves as a role model for taking responsibility to manage own learning and development; seeks feedback and uses other sources of information to identify appropriate areas for personal improvement; targets learning needs and takes action.

Seeks learning activities—Demonstrates motivation for continuous learning; identifies and participates in appropriate learning activities (for example, courses, reading, self-study, coaching, and experiential learning) that help fulfill personal learning needs; values and pursues lifelong learning.

Takes risks in learning—Puts self in unfamiliar or uncomfortable situations in order to learn; asks questions at the risk of appearing foolish; takes on challenging or unfamiliar assignments.

Maximizes learning opportunities—Actively participates in learning activities in a way that makes the most of the learning experience (for example, takes notes, asks questions, critically analyzes information, keeps potential applications in mind, does required tasks); remains open to unplanned learning opportunities, such as coaching from others.

Applies new knowledge or skill—Puts new knowledge, understanding, or skill to practical use on the job; furthers learning through trial and error in practicing new approaches and behaviors.

6. Technology Literacy

Demonstrates an awareness of or comfort with existing, new, and emerging technologies; demonstrates a practical understanding of technology trends; identifies opportunities to leverage technology in order to accomplish learning tasks and achieve business goals.

Key Actions

Demonstrates awareness of technologies—Monitors new developments in technology; stays abreast of current and emerging trends in technology.

Uses technology effectively—Leverages technologies to accomplish business tasks and achieve business goals.

APPENDIX E

Areas of Expertise (AOE) Competency Dictionary

Table of Contents

AOE1: Performance Improvement (PI)

Applies a systematic process of discovering and analyzing human performance gaps; plans for future improvements in human performance; designs and develops solutions to close performance gaps; partners with the customer when identifying the opportunity and the solution; implements the solution; monitors the change; evaluates the results.

Key Knowledge Areas

Successful performance requires knowledge of:

1. Performance improvement processes.
2. Systems thinking and theory.
3. Performance analysis, e.g., business analysis, performance gap assessment, cause analysis.
4. Approaches for selecting performance improvement solutions.
5. Change management theory.
6. Facilitation methods.
7. Project management tools and techniques.
8. Communication techniques and tools, e.g., adapting message to the audience, using a variety of channels.
9. Group dynamics process.
10. How to evaluate the performance improvement solution.

Key Actions

A successful performer:

1. **Identifies the customer**—Identifies the customer and stakeholders; determines all groups affected by the performance issue and ensures that each group has a stakeholder representing it; determines which stakeholders have resources and decision-making authority (i.e., the customer).
2. **Conducts performance analysis**—Identifies business and performance goals by partnering with appropriate clients; compares actual and ideal performance (i.e., establishes a baseline); identifies performance gaps or opportunities; identifies who is affected by the performance gap and conditions that affect performance.
3. **Conducts cause analysis**—Identifies the root causes of a past, present, or future performance gaps; clarifies the real problem underlying the

need for the performance improvement; breaks down the components of a larger whole; examines work environments for issues or characteristics that affect human performance.

4. **Analyzes systems**—Identifies inputs, throughputs, and outputs of a subsystem, system, or suprasystem and applies that information to improve human performance; realizes the implications of solutions on many parts of an organization, process, or individual, and takes steps to address any side effects of human performance improvement solutions; evaluates how organizational politics may affect performance.
5. **Gathers data**—Gathers pertinent information to stimulate insight in individuals and groups through use of general research methods, interviews, and other data-gathering techniques.
6. **Incorporates customer and stakeholder needs**—Partners with the customer/stakeholder to clarify needs, business goals, and objectives; agrees on desired results and gains agreement on how those results can be achieved efficiently and effectively.
7. **Selects solutions**—Recommends appropriate human performance improvement solutions that address the root cause(s) of performance gaps rather than symptoms or side effects; presents recommended changes to the client and helps them assess cost, time, and risk considerations.
8. **Manages and implements projects**—Identifies key sponsors or champions to help ensure successful project implementation; creates a project management plan and ensures stakeholder buy-in while also adhering to cost, schedule, and performance requirements; gathers formative evaluation data.
9. **Builds and sustains relationships**—Builds credibility and trust with the client based on knowledge and understanding of the business; partners and collaborates with the client on an ongoing basis to maintain a sustained business relationship.
10. **Evaluates results against organizational goals**—Assesses how well the results of a human performance improvement solution match intentions; ensures that goals are converted effectively into actions to close existing or pending performance gaps; obtains results despite conflicting priorities, lack of resources, or ambiguity; links human performance improvement to organizational goals.
11. **Monitors change**—Monitors the human performance improvement solutions as they are being implemented; notifies client of any emerging issues and recommends course change/correction.

AOE2: Instructional Design (ID)

Designs, creates, and develops informal and formal learning solutions to meet organizational needs; analyzes and selects the most appropriate strategy, methodologies, and technologies to maximize the learning experience and impact.

Key Knowledge Areas

Successful performance requires knowledge of:

1. Business strategy, drivers, or needs associated with possible learning solutions.
2. Needs assessment approaches.
3. Research methods, including information scanning, data gathering, and analysis.
4. Content knowledge or techniques to elicit content from subject matter experts.
5. Learning theories.
6. Instructional design theory and process.
7. Various instructional methods, e.g., discussion, exercise, self-directed learning.
8. Various delivery options and media, e.g., mobile, online, classroom, multimedia.
9. Existing and emerging learning technologies and support systems, e.g., collaborative learning software, learning management systems, authoring tools, social media.
10. Individual learning modalities, e.g., visual, auditory, kinesthetic.
11. Individual, group, and organizational differences that influence learning and motivation.
12. Assessment methods and formats, e.g., multiple choice, hands-on performance, open-ended response.
13. Legal and ethical issues related to instructional design, including accessibility and intellectual property.

Key Actions

A successful performer:

1. **Conducts a needs assessment**—Identifies organizational objectives and the learning opportunity; identifies target population characteristics and characteristics of the environment; gathers and evaluates resources

and information, analyzes findings, and incorporates or synthesizes information into the design and development process; identifies anticipated constraints or problems affecting design success or failure, such as equipment deficiencies or lack of support; defines basic outcomes of the learning solution to solve the problem or meet the opportunity.

2. **Identifies appropriate learning approach**—Selects learning approaches that best address the needs of the learners and the organization, e.g., formal classroom training versus an informal approach that encourages the use of personal learning networks.
3. **Applies learning theory**—Incorporates sound principles of current learning theory to the practice of instructional design.
4. **Collaborates with others**—Builds partnerships and relationships among the participants (such as IT) in a learning design project and establishes sign-off and approval processes for each step of the design process.
5. **Designs a curriculum, program, or learning solution**—Uses a variety of techniques for determining instructional content; creates or partners with others to plan and design the curriculum, program, or learning solution; designs an experience that enables informal learning.
6. **Designs instructional material**—Selects, modifies, or creates an appropriate design and development model or plan for a given project; identifies and documents measurable learning objectives; selects and uses a variety of techniques to define, structure, and sequence the instructional content and strategies; designs instructional content to reflect an understanding of the diversity of learners or groups of learners.
7. **Analyzes and selects technologies**—Analyzes the characteristics, benefits, and pros/cons associated with existing and emerging technologies, including online learning, blended learning, and informal learning options and their possible application in an instructional environment; considers online learning options such as extended books and lectures, extended community, extended expert access, simulations, and embedded help; selects technologies based on a needs-driven approach in order to accomplish learning goals and objectives.
8. **Integrates technology options**—Integrates existing and emerging technologies to achieve learning goals; integrates new material and technologies with existing learning resources to produce a coherent blended solution.
9. **Develops instructional materials**—Selects or modifies existing instructional materials or develops new instructional materials; conducts

review of materials with appropriate parties, such as subject matter experts, design team, and the target audience; creates logical learning units/objects as appropriate; designs or builds assets (e.g., role plays, self-assessment tests) to support the learning experience and meet objectives as appropriate; develops instructional content to reflect an understanding of the diversity of learners or groups of learners.

10. **Evaluates learning design**—Proactively identifies appropriate evaluation techniques and applies them, such as summative and formative evaluation, the four levels, and usability testing; conducts appropriate test and revision cycles to assess and test the learning design solution and its impact; assesses whether the learning design solution produces positive results, such as a change in learner attitude, skill, knowledge, and/or behavior.

AOE3: Training Delivery (TD)

Delivers informal and formal learning solutions in a manner that both engages the learner and produces desired outcomes; manages and responds to learner needs; ensures that the learning is made available in effective platforms and delivered in a timely and effective manner.

Key Knowledge Areas

Successful performance requires knowledge of:

1. Learning theories.
2. Various instructional methods, e.g., discussion, exercises, self-directed learning.
3. Ways to facilitate informal learning and build learning communities, e.g., leveraging learning platforms and fostering personal learning networks.
4. Various delivery options and media, e.g., mobile, online, classroom, multimedia.
5. Existing and emerging learning technologies and support systems, e.g., collaborative learning software, learning management systems, social media.
6. Facilitation and presentation techniques and tools.
7. Individual learning modalities, e.g., visual, auditory, kinesthetic.
8. Organizational or cultural differences in learning preferences, communication, and classroom behavior.
9. Own personal learning preferences such as preference for lecture or informal learning approaches.

10. Familiarity with content being taught and how solutions address needs (i.e., context).
11. Legal and ethical issues related to training delivery, e.g., obtaining permission for use of materials and giving credit as appropriate.

Key Actions

A successful performer:

1. **Manages the learning environment**—Schedules events and users/participants; selects facilities conducive to learning; prepares agenda/learning objectives in advance; organizes materials and multimedia equipment; arranges room and equipment for optimal learning; provides materials; ensures access and supplies resources for learning users/participants; provides for breaks/refreshments.
2. **Prepares for training delivery**—Reviews participant and facilitator materials prior to delivery; gathers information about the participants and their characteristics; tailors examples and analogies to ensure relevance to participants.
3. **Conveys objectives**—Informs users/participants of the goals and purpose of the learning solution; ensures that learners have a realistic understanding of what the solution can accomplish.
4. **Aligns learning solutions with course objectives and learner needs**—Monitors needs and learning preferences of users/participants to ensure that the learning solutions meet learner and course objectives; responds to feedback from learners and makes adjustments or enhancements to the learning solution based on this feedback.
5. **Establishes credibility as an instructor**—Demonstrates understanding of course content and its relationship to business needs; uses appropriate terminology and relevant business examples; provides useful information when responding to questions; helps participants apply learning to on-the-job situations.
6. **Creates a positive learning climate**—Establishes a learning environment where learners feel safe to try new skills and behaviors, where individual differences are respected, and confidentiality is supported; personally models behavior that is consistent with the goals of the program.
7. **Delivers various learning methodologies**—Facilitates learning by using various learning delivery methodologies that achieve learning objectives and ensure application, including a combination of lectures, role plays, simulations, technology-delivered training, online learning,

and learning technology support tools; encourages informal learning approaches such as the development of personal learning networks; follows facilitator materials to ensure effective and consistent delivery.

8. **Facilitates learning**—Varies delivery style to fit the audience; adapts to the needs of learners and adjusts curriculum as needed; presents information in a logical sequence; uses appropriate visual aids; listens and responds to questions and objections; leverages the knowledge and experience of participants to facilitate learning; manages group dynamics; manages time on learning topics.

9. **Encourages participation and builds learner motivation**—Uses techniques and skills to engage all participants in the learning experience; adapts own style to different learner and group styles; makes effort to "bring in" passive participants; creates excitement and commitment to the learning experience; engages learners by providing opportunities for participation and experimentation in the learning process; capitalizes on participant diversity to maximize learning; builds a collaborative learning environment.

10. **Delivers constructive feedback**—Provides behavioral feedback on learners' performance during or after the learning experience; maintains or enhances learners' self-esteem; supports feedback with specific examples of behavior and possible alternatives for improving performance; provides a balance of positive and constructive feedback; creates opportunities for self-discovery and insight.

11. **Ensures learning outcomes**—Ensures the learning objectives are met; integrates or embeds appropriate performance support and assessment techniques to check learner's understanding and to ensure skill and/or knowledge acquisition, on-the-job application, and intended business results.

12. **Evaluates solutions**—Monitors the impact of learning solution to ensure its effectiveness; summarizes and communicates evaluation results.

AOE4: Learning Technologies (LT)

Identifies, selects, and applies a variety of learning technologies; adapts learning technologies; matches the appropriate technology to the specific learning opportunity or challenge at hand.

Unlike the other Areas of Expertise (AOE), there are no key knowledge areas or key actions for this AOE. Learning Technologies are applied across a variety of Areas of Expertise (AOEs) and in many different contexts.

The following list contains examples of key knowledge areas and key actions which are tightly linked to the identification, selection, adaptation, and application of learning technologies. These are only a sample of what training and development professionals need to know and do to be successful in the field, as it pertains to learning technologies specifically.

Key Knowledge Areas *(Examples)*

Successful performance requires knowledge of:

1. Various delivery options and media, e.g., mobile, online, classroom, multimedia **(Instructional Design).**
2. Existing and emerging learning technologies and support systems, e.g., collaborative learning software, learning management systems, authoring tools, social media **(Instructional Design).**
3. Various delivery options and media, e.g., mobile, online, classroom, multimedia **(Training Delivery).**
4. Existing and emerging learning technologies and support systems, e.g., collaborative learning software, learning management systems, social media **(Training Delivery).**
5. Existing and emerging learning technologies and support systems, e.g., collaborative learning software, learning management systems, authoring tools, social media **(Managing Learning Programs).**
6. New and emerging talent management software solutions **(Integrated Talent Management).**
7. Existing and emerging technologies that enable informal learning and knowledge sharing, e.g., online collaborative workspaces, mobile technologies **(Knowledge Management).**
8. Social learning techniques and technologies **(Knowledge Management).**

Key Actions *(Examples)*

A successful performer:

1. Analyzes and selects technologies **(Instructional Design).**
2. Integrates technology options **(Instructional Design).**
3. Delivers various learning methodologies **(Training Delivery).**
4. Uses talent management systems **(Integrated Talent Management).**
5. Facilitates social learning **(Knowledge Management).**
6. Leverages technology **(Knowledge Management).**

AOE5: Evaluating Learning Impact (ELI)

Gathers, organizes, and analyzes information regarding the impact of learning solutions against key business drivers; presents the information in a way that is meaningful to the organization; uses learning metrics and analytics to inform organizational decision making.

Key Knowledge Areas

Successful performance requires knowledge of:

1. Statistical theory and methods, e.g., descriptive versus inferential statistics.
2. Research design, e.g., experimental versus correlational design.
3. Analysis methods, e.g., cost/benefit analysis, return-on-investment, return on expectations.
4. Learning analytics.
5. Interpretation and reporting of data.
6. Theories and types of evaluations at the program, system, or organizational level.

Key Actions

A successful performer:

1. **Identifies customer expectations**—Works with customers or stakeholders to determine why they are interested in measurement and what they hope to accomplish with the results; clearly defines research questions, expectations, resources available, and desired outcomes of the evaluation project; manages unrealistic expectations.
2. **Selects appropriate strategies, research design, and measures**—Uses customer questions and expectations to guide the selection of appropriate strategies, research designs, and quantitative and qualitative measurement tools; employs a variety of measures and methods to reduce bias and ensure objective conclusions; identifies appropriate sample sizes, data tracking methods, and reporting formats; balances practical implications of rigor, effort, real-life constraints, and objectivity to create a workable approach; identifies information that indicates whether the program is on track.
3. **Communicates and gains support for the evaluation plan**—Summarizes measurement approach into a clear plan that can be communicated to a wide range of customers and stakeholders and linked to business goals; communicates timelines, roles/responsibilities, and identifies other project management needs; gains buy-in for the plan

from key partners; ensures that all parties understand the approach and their responsibilities.

4. **Manages data collection**—Ensures that all data collection methods are applied consistently and objectively; monitors ongoing data collection to ensure that assumptions required for statistical inference are being met; manages and documents data in a format that can be adequately manipulated during the analysis process (e.g., spreadsheets).
5. **Analyzes and interprets data**—Creates summaries of data in a format that can be readily understood and communicated in order to facilitate decision making; adheres to rules of statistical analysis to reduce bias and provide adequate support for conclusions; uses a process of creative inquiry to fully explore the data and all of its possible implications and meaning.
6. **Applies learning analytics**—Uses a variety of human resource data available through integrated talent management platforms to identify where talent development has the greatest potential for strategic impact; uses data to connect learning and development practices to organizational results.
7. **Reports findings and makes recommendations to aid decision making**—Presents information in a way that is both clear and compelling to customers and stakeholders (different customers may require different information); bases recommendations and conclusions on sound analysis methods; clarifies customer questions and the meaning of the data.

AOE6: Managing Learning Programs (MLP)

Provides leadership to execute the organization's strategy; plans, monitors, and adjusts learning and development projects or activities.

Key Knowledge Areas

Successful performance requires knowledge of:

Strategic Knowledge Areas[1]

1. Organization's business model, drivers, and competitive position in the industry.
2. Existing and emerging learning technologies and support systems, e.g., collaborative learning software, learning management systems, authoring tools, social media.
3. Learning information systems.

[1] These are the knowledge areas necessary to lead the learning function as a business unit.

4. Marketplace resources such as learning and development products and services.
5. Principles of management and leadership.
6. Human resource systems and how they integrate, e.g., workforce planning, performance management, employee development, and compensation and rewards.
7. External systems that can affect organizational performance, i.e., political, economic, sociological, cultural, and global factors that can affect the organization's performance in the marketplace.
8. Legal, regulatory, and ethical requirements relevant to Managing Learning Programs, e.g., employment laws and intellectual property issues.

Tactical Knowledge Areas[2]

1. Learning and development projects and programs being administered in the organization.
2. Budgeting, accounting, and financial management.
3. Project planning and management tools and processes.
4. Communication techniques and tools.

Key Actions

A successful performer:

1. **Establishes a vision**—Creates a picture of how the learning function can improve the performance of the business and enable execution of the organization's strategy; partners with business unit leaders to advocate for improving human performance through the learning function.
2. **Establishes strategies**—Develops long-range learning, development, and human performance strategies to implement the vision; understands what drives the business and determines how the learning function can best add value.
3. **Implements action plans**—Converts the learning and development strategies into action plans; balances or reconciles strategy with real-life constraints of the workplace; creates a reasonable timeline that conforms to the expectations of customers/stakeholders.
4. **Develops and monitors the budget**—Ensures budgets are prepared and followed; prepares budget or project reports on a scheduled or as needed basis.

[2] These are the knowledge areas necessary to manage and implement learning projects.

5. **Manages staff**—Recruits, selects, and manages people in the learning function; assigns roles, responsibilities, and projects; conducts performance appraisals; makes compensation decisions.
6. **Models leadership in developing people**—Serves as a role model in own function; provides coaching and mentoring to individuals or groups; supports continuous learning and staff development that enhances performance; builds team capabilities in effectively partnering with line functions to improve business performance.
7. **Manages others**—Directs, assigns, or manages the work of others on the design team to accomplish project goals and objectives.
8. **Manages and implements projects**—Identifies sponsors or champions to help ensure successful project implementation; sources work, budgets, plans and organizes, manages activities, and executes learning design projects.
9. **Manages external resources**—Identifies which training-related activities can be outsourced; determines external resources available for providing learning and development solutions; selects the most appropriate resources for the solution being provided; negotiates and manages contracts with external partners; maintains contact with external partners to ensure effective delivery.
10. **Ensures compliance with legal, ethical, and regulatory requirements**—Ensures that all delivery complies with relevant legal, ethical, and regulatory requirements; monitors compliance and creates reports as needed.

AOE7: Integrated Talent Management (ITM)[3]

Builds an organization's culture, engagement, capability, and capacity through the implementation and integration of talent acquisition, employee development, retention, and deployment processes; ensures that these processes are aligned to organizational goals.

Key Knowledge Areas

Successful performance requires knowledge of:

1. Key components of talent management systems, e.g., workforce planning and talent acquisition, performance management, employee development, succession planning, compensation and rewards, engagement and retention.

[3] Definition was adapted from the ASTD Research publication *Learning's Critical Role in Integrated Talent Management*.

2. Workforce planning and talent acquisition approaches, e.g., estimating future demand, current capability assessment, job analysis, and competency modeling.
3. Career development theories and approaches.
4. Individual and organizational assessment tools.
5. Talent management analytics.
6. New and emerging talent management software solutions.
7. Approaches to maximize workplace diversity.
8. Legal and ethical issues related to integrated talent management.

Key Actions

A successful performer:

1. **Aligns talent management to organizational objectives**—Works with leaders and business unit heads to ensure that talent management supports key organizational objectives; aligns and integrates learning and development with key talent management processes.
2. **Uses talent management systems**—Uses technologies designed to improve talent management processes (for recruiting, developing, training) in order to meet current and future organizational needs; stays current on emerging technologies and understands how they work together.
3. **Equips managers to develop their people**—Develops managers' performance management skills; provides development tools for managers; helps managers promote employee engagement; holds managers accountable for developing talent; enables employees to take responsibility for their own development.
4. **Organizes delivery of developmental resources**—Provides flexible access to multiple vehicles for developing talent, e.g., training, online learning, social media, coaching, job rotation, stretch and expatriate assignments; selects and manages training suppliers and consultants; monitors delivery of solutions to ensure successful implementation; plans and manages resources to ensure adequate coverage.
5. **Promotes high-performance workplaces**—Facilitates recognition and reward of high performance; leverages learning opportunities for improving performance; balances the investment in developing high-potential talent with providing learning and growth opportunities to all employees.
6. **Coordinates workforce and succession planning**—Works with internal clients/stakeholders to design, develop, and implement succession planning or talent mobility programs to fill key positions now and in

the future; aligns succession plans with business needs and goals; uses techniques such as scenario planning and forecasting, job analysis, and competency modeling.

7. **Facilitates the career development planning process**—Provides support for identifying skills, aptitudes, interests, values, accomplishments, career goals, realistic opportunities, and preparing development plans; orchestrates challenging assignments that build skill, knowledge, confidence, and credibility; monitors alignment between success profiles and individual development plans; manages or conducts career counseling sessions.
8. **Facilitates career transitions**—Works with internal customers to provide consulting services and tools to facilitate individual career transitions such as onboarding, job changes, promotions or outplacement; prepares managers to carry out employee terminations.
9. **Supports engagement and retention efforts**—Integrates learning and development opportunities into the organization's retention strategy; measures employee engagement; involves experienced employees in coaching and mentoring programs; recognizes and leverages generational differences.
10. **Implements individual and organizational assessments**—Provides tools and resources to assess individual strengths, development needs, and limits; aggregates data to evaluate organizational capabilities; offers tools for the enhancement of skills and potential; arranges for testing by qualified professionals.
11. **Uses talent management analytics to show results and impact**—Selects measurement and evaluation criteria that reflect business goals; links talent management efforts to key metrics on organizational scorecards.

AOE8: Coaching (CG)[4]

Uses an interactive process to help individuals develop rapidly and produce results; improves others' ability to set goals, take action, make better decisions, and make full use of their natural strengths.

Key Knowledge Areas

Successful performance requires knowledge of:

1. Core coaching competencies.
2. Ethical guidelines and standards of conduct related to coaching.

[4] This information is based on the ICF (International Coach Federation) Code of Ethics and the ICF Core Coaching Competencies. Additional information can be found at ICF's website: www.coachfederation.org.

Key Actions

A successful performer:

1. **Establishes coaching agreement**—Understands what is required in the specific coaching interaction and comes to agreement with the prospective and new client about the coaching process and relationship; identifies how the coaching goals link to enhanced business performance.
2. **Establishes trust and intimacy with the client**—Creates a safe, supportive environment that produces ongoing mutual respect and trust.
3. **Displays coaching presence**—Is fully conscious and creates spontaneous relationship with the client, employing a style that is open, flexible, and confident.
4. **Demonstrates active listening**—Focuses completely on what the client is saying and is not saying to understand the meaning of what is said in the context of the client's desires and to support client self-expression.
5. **Asks powerful questions**—Asks questions that reveal the information needed for maximum benefit to the coaching relationship and the client.
6. **Uses direct communication**—Communicates effectively during coaching sessions and uses language that has the greatest positive impact on the client.
7. **Creates awareness**—Integrates and accurately evaluates multiple sources of information and makes interpretations that help the client to gain awareness and thereby achieve agreed-upon results.
8. **Designs learning opportunities**—Creates with the client opportunities for ongoing learning, during coaching and in work/life situations, and for taking new actions that will most effectively lead to agreed-upon coaching results.
9. **Develops goals and plans**—Develops and maintains an effective coaching plan with the client.
10. **Manages progress and accountability**—Holds attention on what is important for the client and leaves responsibility with the client to take action.
11. **Meets ethical guidelines and professional standards**—Understands coaching ethics and standards and applies them appropriately in all coaching situations.

AOE9: Knowledge Management (KM)

Captures, distributes, and archives intellectual capital in a way that encourages knowledge sharing and collaboration in the organization.

Key Knowledge Areas

Successful performance requires knowledge of:

1. Knowledge management concepts, philosophy, and theory.
2. Knowledge management best practices.
3. Knowledge mapping techniques.
4. Existing and emerging technologies that enable informal learning and knowledge sharing, e.g., online collaborative workspaces, mobile technologies.
5. Social learning techniques and technologies.
6. Primary business processes that support knowledge exchange, e.g., organizational structure, culture, value systems.
7. Business process analysis as it applies to Knowledge Management.
8. Systems analysis and design.

Key Actions

A successful performer:

1. **Advocates knowledge management (KM)**—Develops the KM vision and strategy ensuring it integrates with the organization's business strategy; helps the organization understand the concept and value of effective knowledge creation, sharing, and reuse; assists senior management in building and communicating personal commitment and advocacy for KM; helps promote the knowledge agenda.
2. **Benchmarks KM best practices and lessons learned**—Examines the experiences of other organizations in developing effective and innovative KM solutions and approaches as appropriate; learns from other organizations that leverage their knowledge resources effectively.
3. **Encourages collaboration**—Examines the design of the workplace and social environments to encourage and facilitate knowledge creation, sharing, and innovation; creates knowledge-content activities that contribute to or manage the capture, sharing, and retention activities such as the after action review process; facilitates knowledge-oriented

connections, coordination, and communication activities across organizational boundaries.

4. **Facilitates social learning**—Supports the use of social media to foster learning and development; leverages social media to facilitate learning.
5. **Establishes a knowledge culture**—Facilitates a culture of acceptance of knowledge management; supports innovation; helps break down the barriers between business units, functions, geographic locations, and hierarchical layers, in order to motivate people to share and use knowledge.
6. **Supports the development of a KM infrastructure**—Participates in the development of the organization's knowledge architecture and infrastructure; establishes processes, policies, and procedures for capturing, organizing, using, and maintaining intellectual capital; builds bridges between information systems, training, human resources, and the business units in support of the knowledge network.
7. **Leverages technology**—Assesses, selects, and applies current and emerging information, learning tools, and technologies to support work-related learning and the development of knowledge.
8. **Manages information life cycle**—Manages the life cycle of information from its creation or acquisition through its expiration including organizing, categorizing, cataloging, classifying, and disseminating.
9. **Designs and implements KM solutions**—Assesses the specific knowledge needs of business processes and workers within those processes; identifies knowledge objects that can be handled in the information system; integrates KM into employee's job activities, into key processes, and across communities of practice.
10. **Transforms knowledge into learning**—Assesses organizational learning capabilities; uses knowledge capture and sharing as way to enhance organization-wide learning; facilitates drawing tacit knowledge from experts (knowledge that experts have but cannot articulate) and makes it explicit knowledge so that others can learn it.
11. **Evaluates KM success**—Assesses the effectiveness of KM strategies, practices, and initiatives; measures benefits and progress against goals; establishes metrics to measure how well the organization leverages its intellectual assets.

AOE10: Change Management (CM)

Applies structured approaches to shift individuals, teams, and organizations from a current state to a desired state.

Key Knowledge Areas

Successful performance requires knowledge of:

1. Systems thinking and open systems theory, i.e., organization is an open system influenced by the external environment.
2. Chaos and complexity theory.
3. Action research theory.
4. Appreciative inquiry theory.
5. Organizational systems and culture, including political dynamics in organizational settings.
6. Change theory and change models.
7. Process thinking and design.
8. Communication techniques and tools.
9. Engagement practices to build critical mass.
10. Diversity and inclusion, including managing differences and resolving conflicts.
11. Motivation theories, including empowerment and rewards.
12. Mindset and mental models and their influence on behavior and performance.

Key Actions

A successful performer:

1. **Establishes sponsorship and ownership for change**—Clarifies case for change and desired outcomes; facilitates client sponsorship of expected outcomes; engages stakeholders to build critical mass of support.
2. **Builds involvement**—Involves people to raise awareness and gathers input on the best course of action; helps clients and change leaders build involvement and ownership in the change process; helps clients create a communication plan that generates buy-in and commitment; facilitates effective two-way communications to ensure understanding, commitment, and behavior change.
3. **Creates a contract for change**—Helps clients contract for change, clarify outcomes, and establish realistic expectations for change;

identifies boundaries for change; clarifies relationships, roles, and ethical parameters; creates conditions for success.

4. **Conducts diagnostic assessments**—Determines which data are needed to clarify issues, including stakeholder expectations; collects information to pinpoint initial steps; diagnoses problems as well as perceptions favoring change; assesses current reality against business/ organizational strategy and desired outcomes to define change efforts needed; identifies formal and informal power networks; establishes design requirements for future state.
5. **Provides feedback**—Prepares clients/stakeholders for receiving the results of data gathering and diagnosis; provides feedback to people in position to influence with course corrections on change strategy; articulates what is happening and what needs to happen in a complex system; builds an impetus to support change.
6. **Facilitates strategic planning for change**—Facilitates creation of overall change strategy with sponsor and key change leaders; clarifies what must change, how to minimize the human impact and optimize buy-in; helps identify all technical, organizational, cultural, and people-related change initiatives; shapes the best process and conditions to accomplish results; designs appropriate change process plans to be time efficient and responsive to needs.
7. **Supports the change intervention**—Helps clients design, assess impacts, plan, and implement the change effort and strategy; identifies innovative ways to structure the system; creates new approaches or models of programs as appropriate; offers advice and support for managing complex projects as needed; refines change strategy; supports learning and course correction.
8. **Encourages integration of change into organizational culture**—Fosters shared mindset in support of change; supports alignment of all systems, policies, and processes of the organization to match and support the change; supports integration and mastery of change effort so that it becomes the norm.
9. **Manages consequences**—Creates strategy to reduce human trauma; manages reactions to the change and the unanticipated consequences of the change; surfaces and resolves conflict; helps clients overcome resistance; influences those who react negatively to support the change.
10. **Evaluates change results**—Facilitates information sharing during the change to ensure that results match intentions; collects information about the impact of the change; communicates results and best practices to interested stakeholders.

Appendix F

Action Planning for Organizations

Using the New ASTD Competency Model

Purpose: This job aid is intended for organizations who want to use the ASTD Competency Model for professional development and workforce planning.

Directions: Use this job aid to help you determine how your organization is currently applying the ASTD Competency Model. Then, based on the needs of your organization, determine where additional development should be directed. In the columns below, for each Area of Expertise (AOE), indicate:

1. **Current state** (in the organization): Is this AOE currently implemented in your organization? Indicate yes or no.
2. **Evaluation of current state:** How effectively is this AOE being implemented in your organization? Use this scale: 1 = not effectively; 2 = somewhat effectively; 3 = effectively; 4 = very effectively.
3. **Gaps:** Considering the needs of your organization, could strengthening this AOE have business impact? Indicate yes or no.
4. **Resources:** What resources exist for building or strengthening this AOE? List them. Consider ASTD tools and certification offerings.

Areas of Expertise (AOEs)	Current State	Evaluation of Current State	Gaps	Resources
Performance Improvement				
Instructional Design				
Training Delivery				
Learning Technologies				
Evaluating Learning Impact				
Managing Learning Programs				
Integrated Talent Management				
Coaching				
Knowledge Management				
Change Management				

Appendix G

Action Planning for Individuals

Using the New ASTD Competency Model

Purpose: This job aid is intended for individuals who want to use the ASTD Competency Model for their own professional development purposes. Most notably, it is designed to help individuals identify and create an action plan to close skills gaps.

Directions: Use this job aid to help you apply the new ASTD Competency Model. Complete Parts 1 and 2 of this job aid. Then discuss the results with a mentor, coach, supervisor, or other knowledgeable person who can give you advice on how to build your competencies and Areas of Expertise (AOE) know-how.

Part 1: Foundational Competencies

Directions: Review the list of Foundational Competencies in the left column below. Then, in the center column, indicate how important these competencies are to your present job performance. Use this scale: 0 = not applicable; 1 = not at all important; 2 = somewhat important; 3 = important; 4 = very important.

In the right column, indicate how much need you have for professional development in each competency. Use this scale: 0 = not applicable; 1 = no need for professional development; 2 = some need for professional development; 3 = need for professional development; 4 = much need for professional development.

At the bottom of Part 1, list your priorities for professional development on these competencies.

	Foundational Competencies	How Important to Your Job?					What Are Your Professional Development Needs?				
		0	**1**	**2**	**3**	**4**	**0**	**1**	**2**	**3**	**4**
1	Business Skills	0	1	2	3	4	0	1	2	3	4
2	Global Mindset	0	1	2	3	4	0	1	2	3	4
3	Industry Knowledge	0	1	2	3	4	0	1	2	3	4
4	Interpersonal Skills	0	1	2	3	4	0	1	2	3	4
5	Personal Skills	0	1	2	3	4	0	1	2	3	4
6	Technology Literacy	0	1	2	3	4	0	1	2	3	4
List your priorities for professional development on these competencies.											

Action Planning—Foundational Competencies:

Identify the top two or three priority Foundational Competencies that you are interested in developing or have a need to develop. Next, add your action steps, the timeframe for completion, and the resources or tools needed.

Desirable Competencies	Action Steps	Timeframe	Resources

Part 2: Areas of Expertise

Directions: An Area of Expertise (AOE) is a specialty area. Some T&D professionals are generalists; some are specialists. For each AOE listed in the left column below, indicate in the center column in what areas you work now and in what areas you believe you will work in the future. Check one or both boxes.

Then, in the right column, indicate how important it is for you to build your expertise in each area. Use this scale: 0 = not applicable; 1 = not at all important; 2 = somewhat important; 3 = important; 4 = very important.

At the bottom of Part 2, list your priorities for professional development on these AOEs.

	Area of Expertise (AOE) (In alphabetical order)	Present or Future? (Place check one or both below.)		Importance of Building Your Competencies in Each AOE				
		Present?	Future?	0	1	2	3	4
1	Change Management	☐	☐	0	1	2	3	4
2	Coaching	☐	☐	0	1	2	3	4
3	Evaluating Learning Impact	☐	☐	0	1	2	3	4
4	Instructional Design	☐	☐	0	1	2	3	4
5	Integrated Talent Management	☐	☐	0	1	2	3	4
6	Knowledge Management	☐	☐	0	1	2	3	4
7	Learning Technologies	☐	☐	0	1	2	3	4
8	Managing Learning Programs	☐	☐	0	1	2	3	4
9	Performance Improvement	☐	☐	0	1	2	3	4
10	Training Delivery	☐	☐	0	1	2	3	4

List your priorities for professional development in these AOEs.

Action Planning—Areas of Expertise:

Identify the top two or three priority Areas of Expertise that you are interested in developing or have a need to develop. Next, add your action steps, the timeframe for completion, and the resources or tools needed.

Desirable Areas of Expertise	Action Steps	Timeframe	Resources

Adapting the 2013 ASTD Competency Model to Your Organization

The 2013 ASTD Competency Model is adaptable to suit a wide range of specific organizational and cultural requirements and needs.

Making Customized Decisions

Here is a checklist for making customization decisions.

- Who are the targeted users of your competency model (what are their job roles)?
- What performance level is being targeted (good or outstanding)?
- What is the time horizon for your competency model (present, future, or both)?
- Where will your competency model be used (geographical scope)?
- Why is your competency model being used (for development only, or for all uses such as recruitment, selection, appraisals, promotion, and compensation)?
- What specifics are important to reflect in your competency model (industry, national culture, etc.)?

Tailoring the Model

Here's a four-phase process to help tailor the competency model to suit your particular use or application.

Phase One—Create a Customized Model

First, form a team of individuals and their supervisors who represent the targeted group you expect to use the competency model. Ideally, this group consists of good or outstanding performers.

Second, ask the team to review the ASTD Competency Model and recommend which AOEs (Areas of Expertise) align with your organization's training and development strategy, mission, and specific needs.

Third, set up a series of meetings (perhaps one per AOE) to discuss behavioral indicators (to identify which key actions the performer needs to demonstrate to achieve success). The team's job is to examine, modify, or remove any behavioral indicators that are not appropriate to your organization's culture. You should end up with a very lean, targeted list.

Fourth, using the results of step three, the team should develop a final ideal performer profile appropriate to your corporate or national culture. This final product is your customized rough draft competency list.

Note: At the end of this process, you might choose to conduct a few behavioral event interviews (BEIs) to ground the rough draft in the reality of your workplace. A behavioral event interview is an interview that is used to collect information about past behavior, usually in a structured and prescribed format. Excellent information about BEIs can be found in *Competence at Work: Models for Superior Performance* by Lyle M. Spencer and Signe M. Spencer (1993, Wiley).

Phase Two—Validate Your Rough Draft Model

The purpose of the second phase is to validate the rough draft competency list with the targeted job incumbents, their immediate supervisors, and their stakeholders.

Now that you have a rough draft of your organization's competencies, you can validate its conclusions and recommendations by conducting a series of focus groups, retreats, or surveys. You can also take a multi-rater assessment approach by asking the performer(s) in your target group(s) and their immediate supervisors if the competencies and behavioral indicators are appropriate. You might include other key stakeholders (such as C-suite executives and learners) in this assessment.

Before beginning the validation, develop a cut score. For instance, if raters are asked to review items on a five-point scale on their importance, eliminate anything receiving less than a 4.5 rating. It is better to have fewer competencies and behaviors than too many because this will help users to focus. At the end of Phase Two, you should have a final, reviewed, and validated list.

Phase Three—Get Senior-Level Approval

Once you and your team are comfortable with your final targeted list, present it (if possible) to a formal team of upper management leaders. Clearly, it is essential to secure agreement from all stakeholders that the final list is in alignment with your organization's strategic goals and current and future business needs. It is also helpful to think about how to best communicate it. Consider creating a representative model graphic that depicts the major competency areas at a high level.

Phase Four—Get Set to Use the Model

Review all elements of your organization's human resource system as they relate to training and development practitioners. Pay particular attention to how the competency model will be applied at the outset of the project.

If you're using the competency model for career and skills development alone, then you might develop assessments to discover the strengths and weaknesses of individual training and development practitioners. If you choose to apply the Competency Model more widely, then you will need to incorporate its contents into all elements of your performance management system (recruitment, selection, development, performance appraisals, and promotion).

A Few Customization Caveats

First, note that all elements of the tailoring process should be done in a way that is legally defensible. Different nations have different laws, rules, and regulations governing employment. Be sure to consult legal counsel in your locale to ensure that a particular model adaption is legally defensible.

Second, each step of the tailoring process should be the focus of a communication plan that parallels—and is as robust as—the technical plan.

Third, remember that globally oriented companies may need to review the competency model in different geographical locations or regions around the world in order to localize the content. While the competencies may remain the same, different regional locales may need adjustments in required behaviors such as for use in Africa, the Americas, Europe, Asia, and Oceania. Therefore, you will need to make adjustments for these differences.

Does your organization want to customize the ASTD Competency Model for its own use?

Contact competencystudy@astd.org to obtain written permission to customize or license the Model before you start. The ASTD Competency Model is protected content with all rights reserved.

PROJECT CONTRIBUTORS

Bruce C. Aaron
Bryan Acker
Denise Angerli-Desiderio
Russell Babcock
Jean Barbazette
Jeremy Boles
Paul Briley
Pat Byrd
Andi Campbell
William Curry
Stephanie Daul
Patrick Deery
Sharon Dera
Linda Erickson
Jeanie Filter
Donald Ford
Lisa Gabel
Pat Galagan
Shane Gallagher
Ellen Guise
Emily Hacker
Gregory Hamluk
Lisa Haneberg
Joseph Hare
Renee Hierholzer
Katherine Holt
Todd Hudson
Cindy Huggett
Jim Kirkpatrick
Wendy Kirkpatrick
Candice Kramer
Courtney Vital Kriebs
Kassy LaBorie
Kim Lintz

The individuals listed here contributed their expertise. ASTD would like to thank these individuals and the many others who have contributed to the project.

Felix Lopez
Sardek Love
Shelley MacDonald
Connie Malamed
Jean Marrapodi
Lorin Mask
Anne Mayer
John McDermott
Darcy McDonald
Gigi McKinzie
Warren Metzger
Jay Naumann
Kent Nuttall
Nancy Olson
Ajay Pangarkar
Suzanne Patrick
Stephen Powers
Kristy Presson
Marc Rosenberg
Bruce Runnfeldt
Lou Russell
Kathleen Ryan
Ethan Sanders
Jan Sims
Kris Kern Stark
Jennifer Streeter
Wassim Subie
Lorree Tachell
Phillip Tanzilo
Tamar Truett
Chad Udell
Bob Von Der Linn
Ellen Wagner
Wei Wang
Shari Ward
Travis Waugh
Deadra Welcome
Rich Wellins
Sharon Wingron
Kay Wood
Sue Ziegler
Bob Zimel
Yael Zofi

REFERENCES

ASTD. (2012). *Developing Results: Aligning Learning Goals and Outcomes with Business Performance Measures*. Alexandria, VA: ASTD Press.

ASTD. (2010). *Learning's Critical Role in Integrated Talent Management*. Alexandria, VA: ASTD Press.

ASTD. (2012). *State of the Industry Report*. Alexandria, VA: ASTD Press.

Bernardin, H.J. (2002). *Human Resource Management: An Experiential Approach*. 3rd ed. New York: McGraw-Hill.

Bernthal, P.R., K. Colteryahn, P. Davis, et al. (2004). *ASTD Competency Study: Mapping the Future*, Alexandria, VA: ASTD Press.

Campion, M., A. Fink, B. Ruggeberg, L. Carr, et al. (2011). Doing Competencies Well: Best Practices in Competency Modeling. *Personnel Psychology*, 64, 225–262.

Caruso, K. (2011, May 12). Competency Models: One Size Does Not Fit All, http://web.viapeople.com/viaPeople-blog/bid/53355/Competency-Models-One-Size-Does-Not-Fit-All.

Girard, J., P. Redman, and L. Wallin. (2011). Magic Quadrant for Mobile Device Management Software, http://www.sap.com/campaigns/2011_04_mobility/assets/Gartner Report_MDM_MQ_April2011.pdf.

Gupta, S.R. (2007). *A Quick Guide to Cultural Competency*. Anaheim, CA: Gupta Consulting Group.

IBM. (2012). Leading Through Connections: Insights From the Global Chief Executive Officer Study, http://public.dhe.ibm.com/common/ssi/ecm/en/gbe03486usen/GBE03486USEN.PDF.

ICF, (2011). ICF Core Competencies, http://www.coachfederation.org/icfcredentials/core-competencies.

Johnson, J.M., and H.S. Pennypacker. (2008). *Strategies and Tactics of Behavioral Research*. 3rd ed. London: Routledge.

Kingstrom, P.O., and A.R. Bass. (1981). A Critical Analysis of Studies Comparing Behaviorally Anchored Ratings Scales (BARS) and Other Rating Formats. *Personnel Psychology*, 34, 263–289.

Landy, F.J., and J.M. Conte. (2009). *Work in the 21st Century: An Introduction to Industrial and Organizational Psychology*. 3rd ed. San Francisco: Wiley-Blackwell.

Lloyd, K. Behind BARS: Evaluating Employees with Behaviorally Anchored Rating Scales, http://www.dummies.com/how-to/content/behindbars-evaluating-employees-with-behaviorally.html.

McLagan, P.A., and D. Bedrick. (1983). *Models for Excellence*. Alexandria, VA: ASTD Press.

McLagan, P.A., and D. Suhadolnik. (1989). *Models for HRD Practice*. Alexandria, VA: ASTD Press.

Pinto, P., and J. Walker. (1978). *A Study of Professional Training and Development Roles and Competencies*. Madison, WI: ASTD Press.

Piskurich, G.M., and E.S. Sanders. (1998). *ASTD Models for Learning Technologies*. Alexandria, VA: ASTD Press.

Rothwell, W.J. (1996). *ASTD Models for Human Performance Improvement*. Alexandria, VA: ASTD Press.

Rothwell, W.J., E.S. Sanders, and J.G. Soper. (1999). *ASTD Models for Workplace Learning and Performance*. Alexandria, VA: ASTD Press.

Rothwell, W., and J. Graber. (2010). *Competency-Based Training Basics*. Alexandria, VA: ASTD Press.

Rothwell, W., J. Graber, and D. Dubois. (2013, in press). *The Competency Toolkit*. 2 vols. 2nd ed. Amherst, MA: HRD Press.

Sanghi, S. (2007). *The Handbook of Competency Mapping: Understanding, Designing, and Implementing Competency Models in Organizations*. 2nd ed. Thousand Oaks, CA: Sage.

Schwab, D.P., H.G. Heneman, and T.A. DeCotiis. (1975). Behaviorally Anchored Rating Scales: A Review of the Literature. *Personnel Psychology*, 28, 549–562.

Spencer, L.M., and M. Signe. (1993). *Competence at Work: Models for Superior Performance*. Hoboken: John Wiley & Sons, Inc.

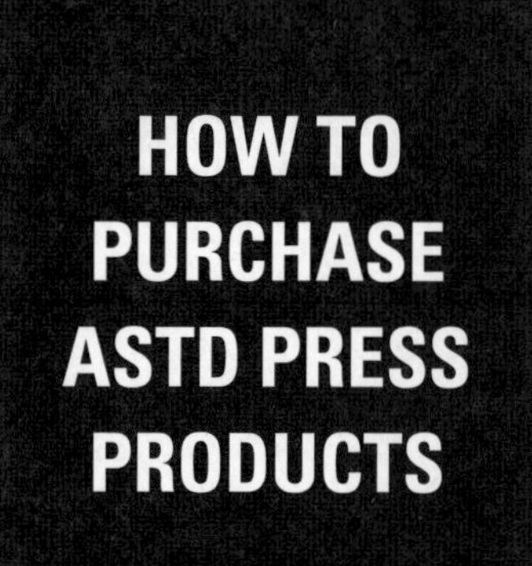

HOW TO PURCHASE ASTD PRESS PRODUCTS

All ASTD Press titles may be purchased through ASTD's online store at **www.store.astd.org**.

ASTD Press products are available worldwide through various outlets and booksellers. In the United States and Canada, individuals may also purchase titles (print or eBook) from:

Amazon– www.amazon.com (USA); www.amazon.com (CA)
Google Play– play.google.com/store
EBSCO– www.ebscohost.com/ebooks/home

Outside the United States, English-language ASTD Press titles may be purchased through distributors (divided geographically).

United Kingdom, Continental Europe, the Middle East, North Africa, Central Asia, and Latin America:
Eurospan Group
Phone: 44.1767.604.972
Fax: 44.1767.601.640
Email: eurospan@turpin-distribution.com
Web: www.eurospanbookstore.com
For a complete list of countries serviced via Eurospan please visit www.store.astd.org or email publications@astd.org.

South Africa:
Knowledge Resources
Phone: +27(11)880-8540
Fax: +27(11)880-8700/9829
Email: mail@knowres.co.za
Web: http://www.kr.co.za
For a complete list of countries serviced via Knowledge Resources please visit www.store.astd.org or email publications@astd.org.

Nigeria:
Paradise Bookshops
Phone: 08033075133
Email: paradisebookshops@gmail.com
Website: www.paradisebookshops.com

Asia:
Cengage Learning Asia Pte. Ltd.
Email: asia.info@cengage.com
Web: www.cengageasia.com
For a complete list of countries serviced via Cengage Learning please visit www.store.astd.org or email publications@astd.org.

India:
Cengage India Pvt. Ltd.
Phone: 011 43644 1111
Fax: 011 4364 1100
Email: asia.infoindia@cengage.com

For all other countries, customers may send their publication orders directly to ASTD. Please visit: **www.store.astd.org**.